QUEEN MARGARET
UNIVERSITY COLLEGE

100 164 132

AP-SS-05

KU-529-708

IMPROVE ◆ YOUR

WRITING

FIFTH EDITION

QUEEN MARGARET UNIVERSITY COLLEGE LIBRARY

RON FRY'S
HOW·TO
STUDY
PROGRAM

IMPROVE·YOUR
WRITING
FIFTH EDITION

by RON FRY

THOMSON
★
™
DELMAR LEARNING

Australia   Canada   Mexico   Singapore   Spain   United Kingdom   United States

THOMSON
DELMAR LEARNING

Improve Your Writing, Fifth Edition
Ron Fry

Vice President, Career Education SBU:
Dawn Gerrain

Director of Editorial:
Sherry Gomoll

Acquisitions Editor:
Martine Edwards

Developmental Editor:
Shelley Esposito

Editorial Assistant:
Paul Carmon

Director of Production:
Wendy A. Troeger

Production Editor:
Joy Kocsis

Director of Marketing:
Wendy E. Mapstone

Cover Design:
Joseph Villanova

Composition:
TIPS Technical Publishing, Inc.

Cover Image:
© Getty Images

Copyright © 2005 Ron Fry
Printed in the United States

1 2 3 4 XXX 07 06 05 04

For more information contact Thomson Delmar Learning, Executive Woods, 5 Maxwell Drive, Clifton Park, NY 12065-2919.

Or find us on the World Wide Web at www.thomsonlearning.com, www.delmarlearning.com, or www.earlychilded.delmar.com

All rights reserved. No part of this work covered by the copyright hereon may be reproduced or used in any form or by any means—graphic, electronic, or mechanical, including photocopying, recording, taping, Web distribution or information storage and retrieval systems—without written permission of the publisher.

For permission to use material from this text or product, submit a request online at http://www.thomsonrights.com

Any additional questions about permissions can be submitted by email to thomsonrights@thomson.com

Library of Congress Cataloging-in-Publication Data

Fry, Ronald W.
 Improve your writing / Ron Fry.—5th ed.
 p.cm.—(Ron Fry's how to study program)

 Includes index.

 ISBN 1-4018-8916-6

 1. Report writing—Handbooks, manuals, etc. 2. Research—Handbooks, manuals, etc. I.
 Title.

 LB1047.3.F796 2005

 808'.402--dc22

 2004008794

NOTICE TO THE READER

Publisher does not warrant or guarantee any of the products described herein or perform any independent analysis in connection with any of the product information contained herein. Publisher does not assume, and expressly disclaims, any obligation to obtain and include information other than that provided to it by the manufacturer.

The reader is expressly warned to consider and adopt all safety precautions that might be indicated by the activities herein and to avoid all potential hazards. By following the instructions contained herein, the reader willingly assumes all risks in connection with such instructions.

The publisher makes no representation or warranties of any kind, including but not limited to, the warranties of fitness for particular purpose or merchantability, nor are any such representations implied with respect to the material set forth herein, and the publisher takes no responsibility with respect to such material. The publisher shall not be liable for any special, consequential, or exemplary damages resulting, in whole or part, from the readers' use of, or reliance upon, this material.

The author and Thomson Delmar Learning affirm that the Web site URLs referenced herein were accurate at the time of printing. However, due to the fluid nature of the Internet, we cannot guarantee their accuracy for the life of the edition.

Contents

Write on!

Reading and organizational skills are the twin foundations of any study program. And preparing a quality research paper requires mastery of both. What it does not require is the ability to write like a pro. In fact, too many students spend far too much time with their thesauruses trying to utilize the most multisyllabic words.

Improve Your Writing *does* talk about writing and will help you improve it. But more importantly, it will help you learn how to organize and communicate your ideas and the fruits of your research. And that is the basis of an A+ paper.

Students must improve their writing, not only to get good grades, but because of a major change looming in the SAT: In March 2005 it will, for the first time, include an essay. So if you have trouble putting sentences and paragraphs together—or spelling them—now's the time to hone your writing skills.

The simple program developed in this book will work for students of any age—not just the high school students I always thought were my readers, but also college students, middle school students, and adults returning to school. All too many of you are parents with the same lament: "How do I get Johnny to do better in school? His idea of researching a paper is skimming the *Cliffs Notes*!"

If you are in high school, I wrote this book with you in mind! While you may have prepared book reports, projects, and short papers in junior high or middle school, you can count on being assigned 10- to 15-page papers with some regularity during high school. And if you're planning to go on to college, I guarantee you must master these skills.

WHAT CAN PARENTS DO?

Writing papers (along with note taking and time management, I think) is one of the skills many teachers seem to assume students can simply learn by osmosis. While term papers are virtually automatic in every English, history, and social studies class from ninth grade up, I've yet to meet many teachers who take the time to teach a good note-taking system, for example, or simple techniques to organize a jumble of notes into a coherent, clearly written paper.

It's up to you to help. That's right, *you*. Don't for a minute underestimate the importance of your commitment to your child's success: Your involvement in your child's education is absolutely essential to his or her eventual success, *even if you were not a great student yourself, even if you never learned great study skills*. You can learn now with your child—not only will it help him or her in school, it will help *you* on the job, whatever your field. Here's a solid game plan for students of any age:

1. **Set up a homework area**. Free of distraction, well lit, with all necessary supplies handy.

2. **Set up a homework routine**. When and where it gets done. Studies have clearly shown that students who establish a regular routine are better organized and, as a result, more successful.

3. **Set homework priorities**. Actually, just make the point that homework is the priority—before a date, before TV, before going out to play, whatever.

4. **Make reading a habit**—for them, certainly, but also for yourselves. Kids will inevitably do what you do, not what you say (even if you say not to do what you do).

5. **Turn off the TV**. Or at the very least, severely limit when and how much TV watching is appropriate. This may be the toughest suggestion to enforce. I know. I'm the parent of a teenager.

6. **Talk to their teachers**. Find out what your kids are supposed to be learning. If you don't know the books they're supposed to be reading, what's expected of them in class, and how much homework they should be scheduling, you can't really give them the help they need.

7. **Encourage and motivate**, but don't nag them to do their homework. It doesn't work. The more you insist, the quicker they will tune you out.

8. **Supervise their work**, but don't fall into the trap of doing their homework. Checking (i.e., proofreading) a paper, for example, is a positive way to help your child in school. But if you simply put in corrections without your child learning from her mistakes, you're not helping her at all...except in the belief that she is not responsible for her own work.

9. **Praise them when they succeed**, but don't over-praise them for mediocre work. Kids know when you're being insincere and, again, will quickly tune you out.

10. **Convince them of reality**. (This is for older students.) Okay, I'll admit it's almost as much of a stretch as turning off the TV, but learning and believing that the real world will not care about their grades, but will measure them by what they know and what they can do, is a lesson that will save many tears (probably yours). It's probably never too early to (carefully) let your boy or girl genius get the message that life is not fair.

11. **If you can afford it, get your kid(s) a computer** and all the software they can handle. There really is no avoiding it: Your kids, whatever their ages, absolutely must be computer-savvy in order to survive in and after school.

12. **Turn off the TV already!**

13. **Get wired**. The Internet is the greatest invention of our age and an unbelievable tool for students of any age. It is impossible for a college student to succeed without the ability to surf the Web, and nearly impossible for younger students. They've got to be connected.

14. **But turn off IM (Instant Messaging) while doing homework**. They will attempt to convince you that they can write a term paper, do their geometry homework, and IM their friends at the same time. Parents who believe this have also been persuaded that the best study area is in front of the TV. (Although they can manage to keep a dozen IM windows going at once. Really.)

SOME RANDOM THOUGHTS ABOUT LEARNING

Learning shouldn't be painful and certainly doesn't have to be boring, though it's far too often both. It's not necessarily going to be painless, either. Sometimes you actually have to work hard to figure something out or get a project done. That *is* reality.

It's also reality that everything isn't readily apparent or easily understandable. Learning something slowly doesn't mean there's something wrong with you. It may be a subject that virtually everybody learns slowly.

A good student doesn't panic when something doesn't seem to be getting through the haze. He just takes his time, follows whatever steps he should, and remains confident that the light bulb will inevitably go on.

Parents often ask me, "How can I motivate my teenager?" My initial response is usually to say, "If I knew the answer to that question, I would have retired very wealthy quite some time ago." However, I think there *is* an answer, but it's not something *parents* can do—it's something you, the student, have to decide: Are you going to spend the school day interested and alert or just sit around being bored and resentful?

It's really that simple. Since you have to go to school anyway, why not develop the attitude that you might as well be active and learn as much as possible instead of being miserable? The difference between a C and an A or B for many students is, I firmly believe, merely a matter of wanting to do better. As I constantly stress in radio and TV interviews, inevitably you will leave school. And very quickly, you'll discover the premium is on what you know and what you can do. Grades won't count anymore, and neither will tests. So you can learn it all now or regret it later.

How many times have you said to yourself, "I don't know why I'm bothering trying to learn this calculus (algebra, geometry, physics, chemistry, history, whatever). I'll *never* use this again!"? Unless you've got a patent on some great new fortune-telling device, you have no clue what you're going to need to know tomorrow or next week, let alone next year or in a decade.

I've been amazed in my own life how things I did with no specific purpose in mind (except probably to earn money or meet a girl) turned out years later to be not just invaluable to my life or career, but essential. How was I to know when I took German as my language elective in high school that the most important international trade show in book publishing was in Frankfurt, Germany? Or that the basic skills I learned one year working for an accountant (while I was writing my first book) would become essential when I later started four companies? Or how important basic math skills would be in selling and negotiating over the years? (Okay, I'll admit it: I haven't used a differential equation in 30 years, but, hey, you never know!)

So learn it *all*. And don't be surprised if the subject you'd vote "Least likely to ever be useful" winds up being the key to your fame and fortune.

THERE AREN'T MANY STUDY RULES

Though I immodestly maintain that my **How to Study Program** is the most helpful to the most people, there are certainly plenty of other purported study books out there. Inevitably, these books promote the authors' "system," which usually means what they did to get through school. This "system," whether basic and traditional or wildly quirky, may or may not work for you. So what do you do if "their" way of taking notes makes no sense to you? Or you master their highfalutin' "Super Student Study Symbols" and still get Cs?

There are very few "rights" and "wrongs" out there in the study world. There's certainly no single "right" way to attack a multiple choice test or to take notes. So don't get fooled into thinking there is, especially if what you're doing seems to be working for you.

Needless to say, don't read my books looking for the capital T Truth—that single, inestimable system of "rules" that works for everyone. You won't find it, 'cause there's no such bird.

You will find a plethora of techniques, tips, tricks, gimmicks, and what-have-you, some or all of which may work for you, some of which won't. Pick and choose, change and adapt, figure out what works for you. Because you are the one responsible for creating your study system, *not me.*

I've used the phrase "Study smarter, not harder" as a sort of catch phrase in promotion and publicity for the **How to Study Program** for 15 years. So what does it mean to you? Does it mean I guarantee you'll spend less time studying? Or that the less studying you do, the better your grades will be? Or that studying isn't ever supposed to be difficult?

Hardly. It means that studying inefficiently is wasting time that could be spent doing other (okay, probably more fun) things and that getting your studying done as quickly and efficiently as possible is a realistic, worthy, and *attainable* goal. I'm no stranger to hard work, but I'm not a monastic dropout who thrives on self flagellation. I try not to work harder than I have to!

It's a Hard-Wired World

In 1988, when I wrote the first edition of **How to Study**, I composed it, formatted it, and printed it on (gasp) a personal computer. Most people did *not* have a computer, let alone a neighborhood network and DSL, or surf the Web (whatever that was), or chat online, or Instant Message their friends, or...you get the point.

In case you've been living in a cave that Bill Gates forgot to wire, those days are very dead and gone. And you should cheer, even if you aren't sure what DOS was (is? could be?). Because the spread of the personal computer and, even more important, the Internet, has taken studying from the Dark Ages to the Info Age in merely a decade.

As a result, you will find all of my books assume you have a computer and know how to use it—for note taking, reading, writing papers, researching, and much more. There are many tasks that may be harder on a computer— and I'll point them out—but don't believe for a second that a computer won't help you tremendously, whatever your age, whatever your grades.

As for the Internet, it has absolutely revolutionized research. Whether you're writing a paper, putting together a reading list, studying for the SAT, or just trying to organize your life, it has become a more valuable tool than the greatest library in the world. Heck, it is the greatest library in the world...and more. So if you are not Internet-savvy (yes, I'm talking to the parents out there, couldn't you tell?), admit you're a dummy, get a book (over the Internet, of course), and get wired. You'll be missing far too much—and be studying far harder—without it.

THE LAST BIT OF INTRODUCTORY STUFF

Before we get on with all the tips and techniques necessary to remember anything you need to, when you need to, let me make two important points about all my study books.

First, while I believe in gender equality, I find constructions such as "he and she," "s/he," "womyn," and other such stretches to be sometimes painfully awkward. I have therefore attempted to sprinkle pronouns of both genders throughout the text.

Second, you will find that many similar pieces of advice, examples, lists, phrases, and sections appear in several of my books. Certainly How to Study, which is an overview of all the study skills, necessarily contains, though in summarized form, some of each of the other five books.

The repetition is unavoidable. While I urge everyone to read all the books in the series, but especially **How to Study**, they *are* six individual books. And many people buy only one of them. Consequently, I must include in each book the pertinent material *for that topic*, even if that material is repeated in another book.

That said, I can guarantee that the nearly 1,000 pages of my **How to Study Program** contain the most wide-ranging, comprehensive, and complete system of studying ever published. I have attempted to create a system that is usable, useful, practical, and learnable. One that you can use—whatever your age, whatever your level of achievement, whatever your IQ—to start doing better in school, in work, and in life *immediately*.

Good luck.

Ron Fry

INTRODUCTION

One Step at a Time

"READING MAKETH A FULL MAN, CONFERENCE A READY MAN,
AND WRITING AN EXACT MAN."
—FRANCIS BACON

There you were, sitting quietly in class, contemplating the upcoming weekend, minding your own business.

Suddenly, without warning, your teacher announces that your next assignment is to write a research paper.

Spending hours in the library or online digging up information, writing a long, detailed report, and typing footnotes—for heaven's sake, if it's not enough to bring on actual terror, it certainly qualifies for mild panic!

"How will I get it all done?" you think. "Where do I start?" and, no doubt, "Why *me?*"

Let me reassure you right off: You will get it done. You will get a great grade on it. You will even learn a few things along the way. How? With the help of this book. I've been there. (And since I'm still writing after all these years, I'm still there!) I'll show you my "tricks of the trade" every step of the way.

Sit in a Straight, Comfortable Chair...

You may have to overcome a few jitters before you start. My guess is that many of you suffer from the same feelings of malaise and procrastination that infected my college dorm when papers were due. Everyone always seemed hell-bent on finding something, anything, that had to be done first...anything, of course, short of actually sitting down and writing that paper. I received this exaggerated but all-too-familiar "paper-writing plan" via email from a colleague's fraternity. Enjoy it (but if you believe this really is the way to write a paper, boy, are we in trouble!).

How to Write a Paper

1. Sit in a straight, comfortable chair in a clean, well-lit place with plenty of freshly sharpened pencils.

2. Carefully read over the assignment. Underline or highlight key instructions.

3. Walk down to the vending machines and buy some coffee so you can concentrate.

4. On the way back to your room, stop and visit your friend from class. If he hasn't started his paper either, watch TV together for a few hours. If, instead, he proudly shows off *his* paper—typed, double spaced, and bound in one of those irritating see-through plastic folders—hurt him.

5. When you get back to your room, sit in a straight, comfortable chair in a clean, well-lit place with plenty of freshly sharpened pencils.

6. Read over the assignment again to make absolutely certain you understand it. Highlight it in a different color.

7. You know, you haven't written to that kid you met at camp since fourth grade—better write that letter now and get it out of the way so you can concentrate.

8. Inspect your teeth in the bathroom mirror. Floss. Twice.

9. Listen to half of your favorite CD. And that's it, I mean it. As soon as it's over start that paper.

10. Listen to the other half.

11. Rearrange all your CDs into alphabetical order.

12. Phone another friend to see if she's started writing yet. Exchange derogatory remarks about your teacher, the course, the university, and the world at large.

13. Sit in a straight, comfortable chair in a clean, well-lit place with plenty of freshly sharpened pencils.

14. Read over the assignment again; roll the words across your tongue; savor their special flavor. Choose at least three more highlighter colors.

15. Check the newspaper listings to make sure you aren't missing something truly worthwhile on TV. NOTE: When you have a paper due in less than 12 hours, anything on TV—from Masterpiece Theater to Rocky & Bullwinkle,—*is* truly worthwhile, with only two exceptions: a) any show involving bowling, and b) any Suzanne Somers infomercial.

16. Study your tongue in the bathroom mirror.

17. Sit down and do some serious thinking about your plans for the future.

18. Open your door; check to see if there are any mysterious, trenchcoated strangers lurking in the hall.

19. Sit in a straight, comfortable chair in a clean, well-lit place with plenty of freshly sharpened pencils.
20. Read over the assignment one more time, just for the heck of it.
21. Scoot your chair across the room to the window and watch the sunrise.
22. Lie face down on the floor. Moan and thrash about.
23. Leap up and write that paper as fast as you can type!

NIBBLES ARE BETTER THAN GOBBLES

A Buddhist saying proclaims that, "The journey of a thousand miles begins with a single step." Well, so does the real process of writing your research paper. The secret is to take things one step at a time. By breaking your assignment—no matter how huge or time consuming a project—into a number of small steps, you'll turn a conceivably immense undertaking into a series of very manageable jobs.

First, in Chapter 1, you'll learn about the different elements that make up a research paper. I'll show you how to put together a work schedule and give you some tips on time management. I'll even tell you what to do if you failed to start your paper soon enough and have 12 days, 8 days, 5 days, or (moan) just a single night to produce one.

In Chapter 2, I'll help you decide on a specific topic…and show you the kinds of topics to avoid like sour milk. I'll also show you how to develop a specific research angle or research argument—your thesis—and produce a preliminary outline for your paper.

Then, in Chapters 3, 4, and 5, we'll spend some time in the library and online. You'll learn where to look for reference materials, a great system for keeping track of those you use, and a special note-taking system. You'll quickly be transformed into a more efficient, organized researcher—and get *more* done in *less* time.

In Chapters 6 and 7, you'll begin the actual writing of your paper. I'll show you some tricks that will help you organize it, some tips on overcoming writer's block—including how to freewrite and brainstorm—and a checklist to make sure you avoid plagiarizing. By the end of Chapter 7, you'll already have written a rough draft. I've also added a new section on preparing lab reports.

In Chapter 8, we'll discuss the various methods you can use to document your sources of information—*when* you must document a source and how to do it.

Next, in Chapter 9, we'll edit your rough draft. You'll learn special strategies that will make your writing better, smoother, and clearer, and why you'll want to spend additional time on the first and last paragraphs of your paper.

You will learn the ins and outs of putting together a bibliography—a list of the reference materials you used to write your paper—in Chapter 10. I'll give you the low-down on all the rules you need to follow, using both MLA (Modern Language Association of America) and APA (American Psychological Association) styles.

In Chapter 11, you'll learn some super proofreading tricks so you catch every typographical error and spelling mistake in your paper. And *voilà*—you'll be on your way to class, finished masterpiece in hand!

In Chapter 12, I've summarized the advice from **"Ace" Any Test** regarding essay tests. Since my advice for such a test is to "Treat it like writing a paper," a short section on essays seemed appropriate for this book. You'll also learn to prepare oral reports.

Finally, in Chapter 13, I discuss Attention Deficit Disorder (ADD), hyperactivity, and the combination condition, ADHD. While these problems concern a minority of you, it is a growing minority. With the help of my good friend Thom Hartmann, author of *Attention Deficit Disorder: A Different Perception* (Underwood Books, 1997), I believe Chapter 13 offers the help these students and their parents need.

You'll thank them later!

Doing a research paper requires a lot of work. But the payoff is great, too. In addition to the obvious benefit— learning a lot about your research subject—you'll develop important skills every step of the way. You will learn, for example:

1. How to track down information about any subject.
2. How to sort through that information and come to a conclusion about your subject.
3. How to prepare an organized, in-depth report.
4. How to communicate your ideas clearly and effectively.

Once you develop these skills, you'll be able to apply them in all your high school or college classes. They'll come in handy not only when you prepare other research papers, but also when you tackle smaller assignments, such as essays and oral reports.

When you graduate, these same skills will help you get ahead in the work world. The ability to analyze a subject and communicate through the written word is a key to success, no matter what career you choose.

Your teacher really didn't ask you to write a research paper just to make your life miserable. Of all the things you'll learn in school, the skills you acquire as we produce your research paper will be among the most valuable.

How to use this book

The steps I outline throughout this book are somewhat flexible. After you've "notched your pen" with one or two papers, you may want to adapt them a bit to fit your personal work style.

That's fine, but *don't skip any step altogether.* You may not understand the benefits of a particular step until you're further along in the process.

Let's get started

Writing a research paper takes time, serious thought, and effort. It is not easy. I can't change that any more than I can change your teacher's mind about assigning the paper in the first place.

But I *can* tell you that if you follow the steps outlined in this book, you'll write a better paper than you ever dreamed possible. It won't be painless, but at least the operation will be a success!

chapter ONE

Getting Ready for Action

● ● ●

Y ou may be writing only *one* paper, but there are actually *three* different jobs ahead of you:

First, you must be an *objective reporter*. You'll dig up all the facts you can about your subject, gathering statistics, historical data, first-person accounts, and more.

You will read reference books, newspaper stories, magazine articles, scholarly journals, and other materials; watch relevant videos or films; check out online resources; maybe even interview an expert or two.

Your job is to find out the truth, to gather data with an unbiased eye. You can't discard or ignore information just because it doesn't fit into the neat framework your personal opinions and expectations have constructed.

Second, you must be a detective. Like a scientist evaluating the results of an experiment, you must review the evidence, decide what it does and doesn't mean, and draw the obvious (and, perhaps, not-so-obvious) conclusions.

Third, you must be an *author*, ready to share your newfound knowledge. Having sifted through reams of information, you will write a cogent, well-thought-out, in-depth report, telling your readers what you have learned.

This is an exciting process—where else can you play three such different roles in a matter of weeks?—but one that demands some organization and adherence to a short, but vitally important, list of rules.

FIVE FUNDAMENTAL RULES

Let's start with the fundamental rules that need to be emblazoned on your mind:

1. *Always* follow your teacher's directions to the letter.

2. *Always* hand in your paper on time.

3. *Always* hand in a clean and clear copy of your paper.

4. Always keep at least one copy of every paper you write.

5. *Never* allow a single spelling or grammatical error in any paper you write.

YOU WANTED IT TYPEWRITTEN?

Your teacher's directions may include:

○   A general subject area from which topics should be chosen—"some aspect of Teddy Roosevelt's presidency," "an 18th-century battle," "one of Newton's Laws" or "a short story by a 20th-century European writer."

○   Specific requirements regarding format.

○ Suggested length.

○ Preferred methods for including footnotes and documenting works consulted (or cited).

○ Other specific instructions.

Whatever his or her directions, follow them to the letter. Some high school teachers may forgive you your trespasses, but I have known college professors who simply refused to accept a paper that was not prepared as they instructed—and gave the poor student an F for it (without even reading it).

At some point, you'll undoubtedly run into a teacher or professor who gives few or no instructions at all. You ask, "How long should the paper be?", and she says, "As long as it takes." Use your common sense. If you're in middle or high school, I doubt she is seeking a 50-page thesis. Likewise, if you're in college, it's unlikely your professor thinks a three-page paper is "As long as it takes." Use previous assignments as a guide.

If you are unsure of a specific requirement or if the suggested area of topics is unclear, it is *your* responsibility to talk to your teacher and clarify whatever points are confusing you.

It is not a bad idea to choose two or three topics you'd like to write about and seek preliminary approval, especially if the assignment seems particularly vague.

Excuses: Nice Try, Bad Grade

There is certainly no reason or excuse, short of catastrophic illness or life-threatening emergency, for you to *ever* be late with an assignment. Some teachers will simply refuse to accept a paper that is late and give you an F for your efforts. At best, they will accept it but mark you down, perhaps turning an A paper into a B...or worse.

TEACHERS DON'T READ COFFEE STAINS

Teachers have to read a lot of papers and shouldn't be faulted if, after hundreds of pages, they come upon your wrinkled, coffee-stained, pencil-written report and get a bit discouraged. Nor should you be surprised if you get a lower grade than the content might merit just because the presentation was so poor.

Granted, the content is what the teacher is looking for, and he should be grading you on what you write. But presentation is important. Teachers are only human (really!), and you can't fault them for trying to teach you to take pride in your work. So follow these simple instructions:

○ Never handwrite your paper.

○ If you're using a computer, put a new ribbon in your dot matrix printer and/or check the toner cartridge of your laser printer. If you type (or have someone else type) your paper, use clean white bond and (preferably) a new carbon ribbon so that the images are crisp and clear.

○ Unless otherwise instructed, always double space your paper. Leave adequate margins all around.

○ Use a simple typeface that is clear and easy to read; avoid those that are too big—stretching a 5-page paper to 10—or too small and hard to read.

○ Never use a fancy italic, gothic, modern, or other ornate or hard-to-read typeface for the entire paper.

RECYCLING ISN'T JUST FOR CANS

There should be a number of helpful messages on your returned paper, which is why it's so important to retain it. What did your teacher have to say? Are her comments applicable to the paper you're writing now—poor grammar, lack of organization, lack of research, bad transitions between paragraphs, misspellings? The more such comments—and, one would expect, the lower the grade—the more extensive the "map" your teacher has given you for your next paper, showing you right where to "locate" your A+.

If you got a low grade but there weren't any comments, ask the teacher why you got such a poor grade. You may get the comments you need to make the next paper better *and* show the teacher you actually care, which could also help your grade the next time around.

TEACHERS DON'T LIKE BAD SPELING

Many employers merrily use resumes and cover letters with grammatical and/or spelling errors for wastebasket hoops practice. Don't expect your teachers to be any more forgiving—there are definitely a few out there who will award an F without even noticing that the rest of the paper is great. It's really too bad you misspelled "Constantinople" or left a participle twisting slowly in the wind.

PAPER WRITING 101

With apologies to the compilers of the "How to Write a Paper" list cited in the Introduction, here are the *real* steps that, with some minor variations along the way, are common to virtually any written report or paper:

1.   Research potential topics.
2.   Finalize topic.
3.   Carry out initial research.
4.   Prepare general outline.
5.   Do detailed research.
6.   Prepare detailed outline (from note cards).
7.   Write first draft.
8.   Do additional research (if necessary).
9.   Write second draft.
10. Prepare final bibliography.
11. Spell check and proofread entire paper.
12. Have someone else proofread.
13. Produce final draft.
14. Proofread one last time.
15. Turn it in and collect your A+.

Doing all these tasks efficiently and effectively requires careful timing and planning. This may not be the only assignment—or even the only paper—you have to finish in a short amount of time.

So get out your calendar and mark the date your paper is due. How many weeks till then? Four? Six? Ten? Plan to spend from one-half to three-quarters of your time on research, the rest on writing.

Block out set periods of time during each week to work on your paper. Try to schedule large chunks of time—at least two or three hours, if possible—rather than many short periods. Otherwise, you'll spend too much time trying to remember where you left off and repeat steps unnecessarily.

As you make up your work schedule, set deadlines for completing the general steps of your paper writing process. For example:

Week 1:   Decide on the topic and "angle" of your paper; make a list of reference materials.

Weeks 2–4: Read reference materials; take notes.

Week 5:   Do detailed outline; write first draft.

Weeks 6–7: Edit paper; prepare bibliography.

Week 8:   Proofread paper; type final copy.

Of course, I can't tell you exactly how much time to set aside for each step, because I don't know any of the specifics about your paper—how long it's supposed to be, how complex the topic—or how fast you work. I *can* tell you that you should plan on consulting and/or taking notes from at least 10 different sources. (Your teacher or subject may demand *more*; I doubt you'll need fewer.) And plan on writing two or three drafts of your paper before you arrive at the final copy.

Refer to your work schedule often, and adjust your pace if you find yourself lagging.

The more time you have to complete a project, the easier it is to procrastinate about dealing with it, even to putting off identifying the steps and working them into your regular schedule. If you find yourself leaving such long-term projects to the last week, schedule the projects furthest away—the term paper due in three months, the oral exam 10 weeks from now—*first*. Then, trick yourself—schedule the completion date at least seven days prior to the actual due date, giving yourself a one-week cushion for life's inevitable surprises. (Just try to forget you've used this trick. Otherwise, you'll be like the perennial latecomer who set his watch 15 minutes fast in an effort to finally get somewhere on time. Except that he always reminded himself to add 15 minutes to the time on his wrist, defeating the whole purpose.)

IF YOU ONLY HAD THE TIME...

Mastering "time management" does not require the brain of a rocket scientist—it just means *making the most of your time*. And that means planning ahead.

Be prepared. Stock up on pencils, typewriter ribbons, computer disks, and any other supplies you need. Otherwise, you may end up running to the store at midnight in search of an elusive printer ribbon or toner cartridge.

One great way to maximize your time is to keep (or have immediate access to) a current reading assignment, your calendar, notes for a project, or all three, with you *at all times*. You'll be amazed at the amount of work you can get done waiting in line, between classes, or any time you have a few minutes to spare.

And stay organized. Keep all materials related to your paper in a separate notebook or file—no messy piles of work scattered here and there, just waiting to be lost or thrown away by mistake.

For a look at "Everything you ever wanted to know" about time management, pick up a copy of **Get Organized**, another of the recently revised books in my **How to Study Program**.

LAST-MINUTE PAPERS

Do not, I repeat, do not put off doing your research paper until the last minute—or even until the last week! If you do, you will make your task much more difficult, and probably wind up with a lousy paper, too. Start working on your assignment now. *Right* now.

Presuming you ignore this command, I am going to be uncharacteristically generous. Here are a few schedules to complete a good paper even if you only have 12, 8, or 5 days before it's due, including how to at least prepare a paper that won't get an F if you have just *one* day.

(I'm sure you've thought of this, but have you asked your teacher for an extension? You just might get it and have enough time to write a decent paper. Unfortunately, this is where your otherwise good study habits will get you into trouble: The better your work in the course, the less likely you'll get a positive response. ["I expect so much more from you, Ron!" Thanks a lot.])

With 12 Days to Go

You've got less than two weeks to prepare a solid paper and haven't even chosen a topic. What do you do? Look back at the 15 steps I outlined earlier in this chapter. Here's how to get them done in the amount of time you have left:

Days 1–2: Determine the topic and "angle" of your paper (steps 1 & 2).

Day 3: Develop a complete list of reference sources and prepare a general outline (steps 3 & 4).

Days 4–7: Read and take notes on all reference materials; prepare your detailed outline; write your first draft (steps 5–7).

Days 8–10: Do any necessary additional research; develop second draft and edit; prepare bibliography (steps 8–10).

Days 11–12: Edit and proofread as many drafts as time permits; print final copy; turn it in! (steps 11–15).

With 8 Days to Go

Day 1:   Determine the topic and "angle" of your paper (steps 1 & 2).

Day 2:   Develop a complete list of reference sources and prepare a general outline (steps 3 & 4).

Days 3–5: Read and take notes on all reference materials; prepare your detailed outline; write your first draft (steps 5–7).

Days 6–7: Do any necessary additional research; develop second draft and edit; prepare bibliography (steps 8–10).

Day 8:   Edit and proofread as many drafts as time permits; print final copy; turn it in! (steps 11–15).

With 5 Days to Go

Day 1:   Determine the topic and "angle" of your paper (steps 1 & 2).

Day 2: (a.m.) Develop a complete list of reference sources and prepare general outline (steps 3 & 4).

Day 2: (p.m.) Read and take notes on all reference materials (step 5).

Day 3:   Prepare your detailed outline; write your first draft (steps 6 & 7).

Day 4:   Do any necessary additional research; develop second draft and edit; prepare bibliography (steps 8–10).

Day 5:   Edit and proofread as many drafts as time permits; print final copy; turn it in! (steps 11–15).

Whenever you have two weeks or less to get a paper together, especially a long or important one, consider teaming up with a study partner. The idea is to share the workload and create two papers more quickly and efficiently than you could write one on your own. This works especially well if the two of you can argue opposite sides of a thesis. The papers will be decidedly different, avoiding any sort of collusion or plagiarism charges, but much of the research will be applicable to both. Talking with each other as you work on your individual papers will undoubtedly hone both your arguments.

BUT MY PAPER'S DUE TOMORROW!!!

Well, you're behind the eight ball now, aren't you? What happened? Did you actually forget to write down when that 15-page history paper was due? Did you keep putting other assignments ahead of it until you suddenly realized it was due tomorrow? Did you decide to run off for a fun weekend even though you *knew* it was due tomorrow?

Well, it doesn't matter how you got here. Here you are. Don't panic. I can show you how to write a paper in only 24 hours. But let's get one thing straight: You're not writing an A+ paper here. So put that fantasy to rest. You're simply hoping not to fail. Here's how you're going to do it.

First and foremost, is there *any* topic on which you are already reasonably well-versed? You really don't have time to start from scratch, so pick a topic you already know something about.

It will help even more if you actually feel passionate about the topic you have chosen. Writing about something that makes you mad or stokes your competitive fires is a lot easier than trying to make a boring topic interesting.

Are there two or three reliable resources—with which you are already familiar—that you can utilize to develop most of your paper? You don't have time to start a Google search and wade through hundreds of Web sites.

Now clear the decks. Writing this paper is all you are doing today. Here's one possible timetable:

7:45 a.m.   Good morning! Eat breakfast.

8:00 a.m.   Determine the topic and angle of your paper, attempting to choose one you already know something about and/or one you are passionate about (steps 1 & 2). Pick two or three trusted references to use (step 3). Do not bother making a general outline (step 4).

9:30 a.m.   Review reference materials; take notes; prepare detailed outline (steps 5 & 6).

10:30 a.m.   Write first draft (step 7).

12:30 p.m.   Eat lunch! You need the break and the fuel.

1:00 p.m.   Fill in the "holes" in your first draft, doing additional research if necessary. Complete second draft. Prepare bibliography (steps 8–10).

4:00 p.m.   Take a break.

4:15 p.m.   Review you paper for logical or grammatical problems and inconsistencies. Rewrite until you are satisfied.

7:00 p.m.   Dinner.

7:30 p.m.   Proofread, print final copy, proofread again (steps 11–14).

11:00 p.m.   Go to bed! You really won't do anything wonderful after already working for nearly 14 hours on this paper! And the more tired you are, the more likely you will fail in the last stage—proofreading—which requires care and concentration.

Last but not least: If you can only compose a decent 10-page paper even though the teacher has asked for 15 pages, take the chance and turn in the shorter paper. Most teachers I know will give you a better grade for a pretty good short paper than for a lousy longer one.

Developing
Your Battle Plan

● ● ●

Y ou're ready to take the first and conceivably most important step on the road to your A+ research paper: choosing a topic.

Once you've chosen a general area of study, you must target a specific topic or question. Then, you need to come up with a general outline—a basic blueprint of your paper.

In this chapter, I'll help you complete all three tasks.

CHOOSING YOUR TOPIC

In some cases, your teacher will assign your topic. In others, your teacher will assign a general area of study, and you'll have the freedom to pick a specific topic.

With freedom sometimes comes danger—give this decision long and careful thought. Pick the wrong topic, and you can write yourself right into disaster.

I'm not implying that you should pick the simplest topic you can find—simple topics often lead to simply awful papers—but there are definitely pitfalls you must avoid.

Danger #1: Thinking Too Big

You need to write a 15-page paper for your history class and decide your topic will be "The Presidency of Ulysses S. Grant."

Whoa, Nelly! Think about it: Can you really cover a topic that broad in 15 pages? Not unless you simply rehash the high points. You could write volumes on the subject (people have) and still have plenty left to say!

Instead, you need to focus on a particular, limited aspect of such a broad subject or attack it from a specific angle. How about "The Major Scandals of the Grant Presidency"? That would work for a middle school or high school paper. For college, you would probably want to focus on a single scandal.

Remember, your job is to prepare an *in-depth* report about your subject. Be sure you can do that in the number of pages your teacher has requested.

Danger #2: Thinking Too Small

By the same token, you must not focus too narrowly. Choose a subject that's too limited, and you might run out of things to say on the second page of your paper. "Why U.S. Grant Drank" might make a humorous 1- or 2-page essay, but it won't fill 10 or 15 pages...even with really wide margins.

Hint: If you can't find a single book on your supposed topic, rethink it! While there's nothing wrong with choosing a topic that can be researched via magazine articles, the newspaper, the Internet, and the like, why make your research so difficult if you don't have to?

Danger #3: Trodding the Lonesome Trail

Pick a topic that's too obscure, and you may find that little or no information has been written about it. In that case, you will have to conduct your own experiments, interview your own research subjects, and come up with your own original data. That is, of course, how scientists forge new pathways into the unknown. But I'm guessing that you have neither the time, desire, nor experience to take a similar start-from-scratch approach.

Take it from someone who's done this more than once—it may be wonderfully creative and a lot of fun to work in such original areas, but it can also be frustrating and stressful. And don't underestimate the reaction of your teacher, who may well wish for something a little easier to grade than some far-reaching new theory he or she really needs to think about. I got a C on the best paper I think I ever wrote. The grad student grading it came right out and told me that since he couldn't "check" my ideas—there was nothing published to support my interpretation—he couldn't give me a better grade. I think that attitude was absurd—and that the C was, too—but I suggest you keep it in mind.

Don't bite off more than you can chew, but make sure there's *something* to gnaw on! And make sure that there are enough *different* sources of material—different authors, different books, and so on—so you can get a well-rounded view of your subject (and not be forced, for lack of other material, to find ways to make somebody else's points sound like your own).

MAKE A POSSIBILITIES LIST

Taking all of the above into consideration, do a little brainstorming now about possible topics for your paper. Don't stop with the first idea—come up with several different possibilities.

In fact, put this book down and go make a list of three or four potential topics right now.

(If you really want a special Fry award for forward thinking, how about trying to get two or more papers for two or more classes *out of the same research*? At the very least, you should be able to do a little extra research—not what you would expect to do for an entirely different paper—and utilize a good portion of the first paper as the basis for a second. What a great way to maximize your research time!)

If you are absolutely at a loss, here are two books that will help:

10,000 Ideas for Term Papers, Projects, Reports and Speeches: Intriguing, Original Research Topics for Every Student's Need, 5th Edition, by Kathryn Lamm (Arco, 1998).

1001 Ideas for English Papers: Term Papers, Projects, Reports and Speeches by Walter James Miller (Hungry Minds, Inc., 1994).

While older (and, I suspect, already integrated into Lamm's book), here are some other potential idea sources:

1000 Ideas for Term Papers in American History by Robert Allen Farmer (Arco, 1969).

1000 Ideas for Term Papers in Philosophy and Religion by Brother Uttal (Arco, 1973).

1000 Ideas for Term Papers in Social Science
by Robert Allen Farmer (Arco, 1970).

1000 Ideas for Term Papers in World Literature
by Robert Allen Farmer (Arco, 1970).

Do SOME PRELIMINARY RESEARCH

Got your list? Then get thee to a library. You need to do
a little advance research.

Scan your library's card-catalog index or computer listings, the *Readers' Guide to Periodical Literature*, and other
publication indexes. How many books and articles have
been written about each topic on your "possibilities" list?
Read a short background article or encyclopedia entry
about each topic.

Alternatively, spend a little time online. Are there specific Web sites devoted to your topic? Lucky you! Or does
a keyword search result in 10,424 matches, none of which
has a *thing* to do with your topic?

By the time you leave the library or go offline, you
should have a general understanding of each of your potential subjects. You also should know whether you'll have
trouble finding information about a topic on your list. If so,
eliminate it.

And THE WINNER IS (DRUMROLL, PLEASE)...

With any luck at all, you should be left with at least one
topic that looks like a good research subject. If two or
more topics passed your preliminary research test, pick
the one that interests you most.

You're going to spend a lot of time learning about your subject. There's no rule that says you can't enjoy it!

Develop a Temporary Thesis

Once you have chosen the topic for your paper, you must develop a *temporary thesis*.

What's a *thesis*, you ask? The word "thesis" is a relative of "hypothesis"—and means about the same thing: the central argument you will attempt to prove or disprove in your paper. It's the conclusion—based upon your research—you draw about your subject.

A thesis is not the same thing as a *topic*. Your topic is what you study; your thesis is the conclusion you draw from that study.

A *thesis statement* is a brief summary of your thesis, summing up the main point of your paper.

Suppose you decided to actually do a paper on "The Major Scandals of the Grant Presidency." Your thesis statement might be: "Although the hero of Vicksburg was the first President to confront serious charges of wrongdoing during his term of office, Grant himself was never directly associated with any involvement in criminal acts. Nevertheless, suffering through four major scandals during two terms set a disturbing precedent for administrations to come."

Temporary Means Just That

Note that word temporary. No matter how good it looks to you now, your temporary thesis may not wind up being your final thesis. Because you haven't completed all your research yet, you can only come up with a "best guess" thesis at this point.

You may find out during your research that your temporary thesis is all wet. If that's the case, you will revise it, perhaps even settling on a thesis that's the exact opposite of your first! In fact, you may revise your thesis *several* times during the course of your research.

If a temporary thesis doesn't spring easily to mind—and it may not—sit back and do some more brainstorming. Ask yourself questions like (fill in the blank with your topic.):

"What's special or unusual about _____?"

"How is _____ related to events in the past?"

"What impact has _____ made on society?"

"What do I want the world to know about _____?"

"What questions do I have about _____?"

The answers to these and similar questions should lead to several good thesis ideas. If you find yourself needing more information about your topic to answer these questions, do more research.

ASK YOUR INSTRUCTOR

Some teachers require you to submit your thesis statement for their approval prior to beginning your paper. Even if this is not required, getting your instructor's opinion is always a good idea. He or she will help you determine whether your thesis argument is on target and, if not, perhaps how to fix it.

CREATE A TEMPORARY OUTLINE

Once you have developed your temporary thesis, think about how you might approach the subject in your paper. Jot down the various issues you plan to investigate. Then come up with a brief, temporary outline of your paper, showing the order in which you might discuss those issues.

Based on your preliminary research, your general, temporary outline of your President Grant paper might look like this:

     I.   Black Friday.

    II.   Credit Mobilier affair.

   III.   The Whiskey Ring.

   IV.   The Belknap bribery.

    V.   Effect of scandals on Grant's presidency.

   VI.   Comparison with later presidential scandals.

Don't worry too much about this outline—it will be brief, at best. It's simply a starting point for your research, a plan of attack.

But don't skip this step, either. As you'll find out in later chapters, it will be a big help in organizing your research findings.

Your Approach to Research

● ● ●

Getting the right start is crucial. Since I try to keep from being overwhelmed with too much material, I begin any research working with the broadest outlines or topics (and the broadest resources) and slowly narrow my focus, getting more and more specific in topic and sources as I go along.

So start with any one of the numerous leading encyclopedias in your library or online—Britannica, Americana, Collier's, World Book, and so forth. Encyclopedic entries are usually the most comprehensive and concise you will find. They cover so much territory and are so (relatively) up to date that they are an ideal "big picture" resource.

And don't forget to seek out a subject-specific encyclopedia. It seems there is such a tome on anything you can think of, to wit: *Encyclopedia of Christmas, Charlie Chan Film Encyclopedia, Encyclopedia of Paleontology,*

Encyclopedia of the Renaissance, Dictionary of Theology, A History of Women's Writing in France, Encyclopedia of Deserts, Encyclopedia of the Solar System, Encyclopedia of Human Nutrition, Encyclopedia of Smoking and Tobacco, Historical Encyclopedia of Nursing, and the *Oxford Companion to Food*.

If you are writing a paper about a historical or contemporary figure, also consider skimming a biographical dictionary or, even better, one of the specific volumes in the *Who's Who* series, which ranges from *Who's Who in Art* and *Who's Who in American Jewry* to *Who's Who in Vietnam* and *Who's Who in Theatre*.

Needless to say, new CD-ROMs and reference Web sites appear almost hourly. These many current resources should make it increasingly easy to choose a good topic, establish a reasonable thesis, and gather enough information to construct an initial outline, without having to do any further research.

But completing an A+ paper will still require you to turn to other sources for more detailed information. You need to read books written by experts in the field you're researching, as well as magazine and newspaper articles about every aspect of your subject.

Why stop there? Pamphlets, anthologies, brochures, government documents, films, and videos are just some of the other possible sources of information for your paper.

WHERE TO LOOK FOR MATERIALS

How do you find out whether anyone has written a magazine or newspaper article about your topic? How do you know if there are any government documents or pamphlets that might be of help? How do you locate those written-by-the-experts reference books?

You look in your library's publication indexes, which list all of the articles, books, and other materials that have been published and/or are available in your library. Most are arranged alphabetically by subject:

1. **The card catalog**. This is a list of all the books in your library. (Although many libraries now store it on computer, it's still often called a card catalog because it used to be kept on index cards.) Books are indexed in three different ways: by subject, by author, and by title.

2. **Book catalogs**, the best-known of which are Books in Print, Forthcoming Books, and the Cumulative Book Index.

3. **Newspaper indexes**. Several large city newspapers provide an indexed list of all articles they have published. Your library may even have past issues of one or more available on microfiche.

4. **Periodical indexes**. To find out if any magazine articles have been published on your subject, go to a periodical index. The *Readers' Guide to Periodical Literature*, which indexes articles published in the most popular American magazines, may be one with which you're already familiar.

5. **Vertical file**. Here's where you'll find pamphlets and brochures.

6. **Guide to U.S. Government Publications, American Statistical Index, and Congressional Information Service Index**. These are all useful for locating government publications.

7. **Computer databases**. Widely used indexes are available covering American and world history, art, biology, philosophy, religion, psychology, engineering, and much more.

8. **The Internet**. Most magazines, newspapers, encyclopedias, government organizations, and so forth
   have Web sites that can be a starting point for your
   search. They often have links to other sites where
   you can find full-length articles and stories, bio-
   graphic information, and the like.

How your library is organized

To provide organization and facilitate access, most small
and academic libraries utilize the Dewey decimal classification system, which uses numbers from 000 through 999
to classify all material by subject matter. It begins by
organizing all books into 10 major groupings.

Given the millions of books available in major
libraries, just dividing them into these 10 groups would
still make it quite difficult to find a specific title. So each
of the 10 major groupings is further divided into 10, and
each of these now 100 groups is assigned to more specific
subjects within each large group. For example, within the
philosophy classification (100), 150 is psychology and 170
is ethics. Within the history classification (900), 910 is
travel and 930 is ancient history.

000–099	General
100–199	Philosophy
200–299	Religion
300–399	Social Sciences
400–499	Language
500–599	Natural Science and Mathematics
600–699	Technology
700–799	Fine Arts

| 800–899 | Literature |
| 900–999 | General Geography and History |

There is even further subdivision. Mathematics is given its own number in the 500 series—510. But specific subjects within mathematics are further classified: 511 is arithmetic, 512 is algebra, and so on.

Finally, to simplify your task even more, the last two digits in the Dewey code signify the type of book:

01   Philosophy of

02   Outlines of

03   Dictionary of

04   Essays about

05   Periodicals on

06   Society transactions and proceedings

07   Study or teaching of

08   Collections

09   History of

If your library doesn't use the Dewey system, it probably is organized according to the Library of Congress system, which uses letters instead of numbers to denote major categories:

A: General works
(encyclopedias and other reference)

B: Philosophy, Psychology, and Religion

C: History: Auxiliary sciences
(archeology, genealogy, etc.)

D: History: General, non-American

E: American history (general)

F: American history (local)

G: Geography/Anthropology

H: Social sciences
      (sociology, business, economics)

J: Political sciences

K: Law

L: Education

M: Music

N: Fine arts (art and architecture)

P: Language/Literature

Q: Sciences

R: Medicine

S: Agriculture

T: Technology

U: Military science

V: Naval science

Z: Bibliography/Library science

USING ONLINE RESOURCES

There's so much material on the Internet, it's easy to be overwhelmed. While it can be extremely helpful to have access to some obscure Web sites that have just the material you need, especially when a book or two you want to take notes from has disappeared from the library, I am still convinced that most of you will waste too much time if the majority of your research is done online. I can attest from far too much personal experience that it is ridiculously easy to get sidetracked when doing research online. "Wow, I didn't know there were that many cool sites about bungee jumping. I'd better check them out...right now!"

Be careful about the following two things:

While much of the "basic" information on most research-oriented Web sites is not going to radically change day to day, that is certainly not true of all sites. Just as the identical keyword search may yield radically different results if run on two separate days (or on two different search engines), you may find material you needed deleted the next time you look for it. So if you find something really good, download it, save it to your hard drive, or print a hard copy.

Anyone can post information on the Web, whether they're qualified or not, whether the material is accurate or not. Make sure your sources are reputable so your teacher doesn't question the validity of your information.

Virtually all of the widely used periodical indexes—covering American and world history, art, biology, philosophy, religion, psychology, engineering, and much more—are available on the Web. And most magazines, newspapers, encyclopedias, government organizations, and so forth have their own Web sites.

Online bookstores (amazon.com, bn.com, and, if you're Canadian, chapters.indigo.ca) will list many books even before they're published, and almost always before your local library has ordered, cataloged, and shelved them. Amazon's recently added feature of including searchable pages from many titles—from a table of contents and a short excerpt to 50 pages of text or more—should help you get a feel for whether the book or a portion of it is pertinent to your topic.

Amazon in particular offers a "People who bought this book also bought" feature, a good way to locate related resources (especially since none of the online bookstores make searches by subject easy or accurate).

AN APPROACH TO ONLINE RESEARCH

I am indebted to Robin Rowland, author of *The Creative Guide to Research* (Career Press, 2001), for the following suggestions on how to maximize your time online:

○ Long before a paper is due, choose four search engines—one a meta-search engine (which searches other search engines), the other three regular. Robin's recommendations: Copernic (meta), Google, Hotbot, AltaVista, Northern Light, Dogpile (meta).

○ When beginning your research, use the meta engine first.

○ Learn each engine's advanced features—you'll find things faster and easier.

○ Print out the FAQ pages for each search engine and create your own manual.

○ Choose three search engines with different strengths to maximize your search abilities.

○ Consider using a specialized search engine, such as Beaucoup, if you are unable to find what you want or have found too much information.

○ Learn Boolean searches.

There's no room in this book to list even a smattering of pertinent Internet sites. Wherever you go on the Net, just remember:

○ Some of the sites are informative and well-organized; some are quirky and skimpy.

○ Some are well-researched and trustworthy; some are the rantings of a mad person. Just because something is on your computer screen doesn't mean it's true.

○ Some provide unbiased information with no ulterior motive; some slant their information to sell you on their cause. Some are offering information just to entice you to buy something.

○ Some are easy to use; some require you to search through listings to find what you need.

○ Some supply information; some link you to other sites; some are simply listings of sites.

○ Some may be gone when you look for them again.

○ Some are free; some cost a bit...some cost a lot. Be sure to check out the cost before using a site where you have to pay.

Creating a
Working Bibliography

●　●　●

Working bibliography? "Ugh," you think, "sounds complicated. Sounds like work!"

Relax. Remember what I told you in Chapter 3—the first step of your research is to put together a list of books, magazines, newspapers, and Web sites you plan to consult. "Working bibliography" is simply a fancy name for that list.

There are two steps involved. First, you'll create bibliography cards for each source you want to review. Then, you'll transfer all the information from your bibliography cards to a single list—your working bibliography.

This two-step method has been around since someone wrote the first research paper, and with good reason: It works! It helps you conduct your research in an organized, efficient manner *and* makes preparing your final bibliography easier.

In other words, this is one of those great time-saving tools that I promised to show you! This is not a complicated job, but it is an important one.

ESSENTIAL INGREDIENTS: 3 X 5 INDEX CARDS

To create your bibliography, you'll need a supply of 3 x 5 index cards. You can buy these for next to nothing at most dime stores, bookstores, and office stores. (You'll also use index cards when you take notes for your paper, so buy a big batch now. A few hundred cards ought to suffice.)

While you're stocking up on index cards, pick up one of those little boxes designed to hold the cards. Put your name, address, and phone number on the box. If you lose it, some kind stranger may return it. If not, after you duplicate all your work, I guarantee you'll never lose one again.

Step 1: Create Your Bibliography Cards

Start a systematic search for any materials that might have information related to your paper. When you find a book, article, Web site, or other resource that looks promising, take out a blank note card. On the front of the card, write down the following information:

In the upper right-hand corner of the card: Write the library call number (Dewey decimal number or Library of Congress number), if there is one, or the complete URL. Add any other detail that will help you locate the material on the library shelves (e.g., Science Reading Room, Reference Room, Microfiche Periodicals Room). And make sure to write down the *complete* Web address.

On the main part of the card: Write the author's name, if given—last name first, followed by first name, then middle name or initial. Then the title of the article, if applicable, in quotation marks. Then the name of the book, magazine, newspaper, Web site, or other publication—underlined. (If you've already written the complete Web address in the right-hand corner of the card, you do not need to duplicate it.)

Add any details you will need if you have to find the book or article again, such as:

○ Date of publication.

○ Edition—e.g., "third (1990) edition" for a book; "morning edition" for a newspaper.

○ Volume and/or issue number.

○ Page numbers on which the article or information appears.

Again, it is essential to write down the exact and complete Web address, not just that of the main Web site. Navigating a complex site to find that short quote you wrote down can waste a lot of time.

In the upper left-hand corner of the card: Number it. The first card you write will be #1, the second, #2, and so on. If you happen to mess up and skip a number somewhere along the line, don't worry. It's only important that you assign a different number to each card.

Do this for *each* potential source of information you find, and *put only one resource on each card*.

Some experts in the research paper business have different ideas about what goes where on bibliography cards. It's not really important—if you prefer to put the elements of your card in some different order, do so.

Just be sure that you're consistent, so you'll know what's what later on. And leave some room on the card— you'll be adding more information later.

Sample Bibliography Card for a Book

1   315.6 Main Reading Room Spechler, Jay W. Reasonable Accommodation: Profitable Compliance with the Americans with Disabilities Act (see esp. pp. 54–61) Computer Card Catalog College Library

Sample Bibliography Card for a Magazine Article

2   www.timeinc.com/pub/2003/index.html Smolowe, Jill "Noble Aims, Mixed Results" *Time* (July 31, 2003; pp. 54–55)

Sample Bibliography Card for a Newspaper Article

3   www.nytimes/index/404/5.html Wade, Betsy "Disabled Access to Inns at Issue" *The New York Times* (April 14, 2004, section 5, page 4)

Citing Online Information

Because students are increasingly using online sources, the MLA and APA, which publish style guides for research papers, have integrated electronic citations into their latest editions.

The MLA does not publish its documentation guidelines on the Web. The *MLA Handbook for Writers of Research Papers* by Joseph Gibaldi (for high school and undergraduate college students) is now available in a sixth edition (2003). The *MLA Style Manual and Guide to Scholarly Publishing, 2nd Ed.* (1998), also by Gibaldi, is for graduate students, scholars, and professional writers. *The Publication Manual of the APA, 5th Ed.* (2001) is also not available for free on the Web, but detailed examples can be found at a number of addresses.

Another good source to consult is *Research and Documentation in the Electronic Age* by Diana Hacker (Bedford/St. Martins, 2003), which details citations using both styles.

Here is a sample online citation:

Furfaro, John P. and Maury B. Josephson. "Reasonable Accommodation to Disability Act." *New York Law Journal.* http://homepages.go.com/~atlanticcity/040299 c4.htm (2 April 1999)

Evaluating Resources

You may find so many potential resources that you won't have time to read them all. Concentrate on those that have been published most recently or written by the most respected sources. However, don't limit yourself *too* much —gather information from a wide range of sources. Otherwise, you may learn only one side of the story.

There are two types of resources: *primary* and *secondary.*

Primary resources are written by people who *actually witnessed or participated in an event*. When you read a scientist's report about an experiment he has conducted, you are consulting a primary resource.

Secondary resources are written by people *who were not actually present at an event*, but have studied the subject. When you read a book about the 1950s written by someone who was born in 1960, you are learning from a secondary resource.

Primary resources are likely to be more reliable sources of information. But depending upon your subject, there may not be any primary resources available to you.

Step 2: Prepare Your Working Bibliography

Copy the information from each of your bibliography cards onto a single list. As you do this, follow the bibliography style rules outlined in Chapter 10. I have included samples of both MLA and APA formats for a wide variety of resources. (These rules cover bibliographic minutiae—where to put periods, how many spaces to indent lines, and so forth.) When you have finished your list—your working bibliography—make a photocopy or two. Keep one copy with your research file, another in a safe place in your room or desk.

Although you'll work from your bibliography cards as you conduct your research, your working bibliography is important for two reasons:

1. You'll have a separate record of all the potential resources you found. If you lose any of your bibliography cards, you will still have all the information about the source.

2. You'll be able to use your working bibliography as the basis for your final one.

The final bibliography, a required part of your paper, lists resources from which you gathered information. Your *working* bibliography contains all the resources from which you *might* gather information.

LOOKS LIKE EXTRA WORK TO ME!

Why bother to create all those bibliography cards if you're just going to transfer the information to another piece of paper? Can I possibly be wasting your time? Of course not. It's a matter of convenience and organization.

With index cards, you can organize your list of resources in different ways, just by shuffling the deck.

For example, you might want to start by organizing your cards by resource: magazine articles, encyclopedias, books, newspapers, Web sites, and so forth. Then, when you're in the magazine room of the library, you will have a quick and easy way to make sure you read all your magazine articles at the same time. Ditto for your trip to the newspaper reading room, the reference shelf, and so on.

But at some point, you might want to have your list of resources organized in alphabetical order, or separated into piles of resources you've checked and those you haven't. No problem: Just shuffle your cards again.

This is one of the few cases where computer literacy can lead you to grief. Do not try to keep your notes—or even your bibliographic cards—on your computer, even if you're using computer-created note cards. It is simply not as easy, neat, or efficient. Trust me. Been there. Done that. Wouldn't be prudent.

Digging in: Researching in Detail

I f you ever thought being a detective or investigative reporter would be fun, then get ready to enjoy yourself! It's time to follow up all of those research leads you found, track down the evidence, and uncover the truth, the whole truth, and nothing but the truth.

In other words, it's time to start taking notes.

When you write your paper, you'll work from your notes, not the original reference materials. Why? Because it's easier to turn a few cards than flip through hundreds of pages or a dozen open computer windows in search of the information you need.

In this chapter, I'm going to show you my own special system for taking notes. Master it—it will be a huge help when you sit down to organize and write your paper.

SEND FOR INFORMATION/ SCHEDULE INTERVIEWS

Before you do anything else, send away for anything you want to review that you can't find in your library or get online. If you want a brochure from a particular association, for example, order it now. It may take a few weeks for such materials to arrive. (Most of the material you need should be easily downloadable from *somewhere*, but there are always exceptions.)

If you're going to interview any experts, schedule interview dates with them. Make up a list of good questions and buy or borrow a quality tape recorder so you can accurately record your interviewee's comments.

THEN HIT THE BOOKS

Set aside solid blocks of time for your research. And remember: It's better to schedule a handful of extended trips to the library than 15 or 20 brief visits, better to do a solid few hours online than 10 minutes here and 15 minutes there.

What sort of information should you put in your notes? Anything related to your subject, and especially to your thesis. This includes:

1. General background information—names, dates, historical data.
2. Research statistics.
3. Quotes by experts.
4. Definitions of technical terms.

You may be used to keeping your notes in a three-ring binder or notepad. I'm going to show you a note-taking system I think is better—you'll record all of your notes on your blank index cards.

As was the case with your bibliography cards, you must follow some specific guidelines to make this method work. You'll want to refer to the guidelines in this chapter often during your first few note-taking sessions. After that, the system will become second nature to you.

Step #1: Complete the Bibliography Card

Let's say that you have found a reference book that contains some information about your subject. Before you begin taking notes, get out the bibliography card for that book.

First, check that all of the information on your card is correct. Is the title exactly as printed on the book? Is the author's name spelled correctly?

Next, add any other information you will need to include in your final bibliography. The type of information you need to put on your bibliography card depends on two factors: 1) the type of reference material, and 2) the bibliography format you are required to use.

Be sure to ask your instructor which style she wants you to follow. The MLA guidelines are probably the "default"—use them unless another system is specified. The MLA guidelines are used primarily for papers in the arts and humanities. If you are doing a paper for a social or behavioral science class, you will probably be instructed to use APA style. Specific—and different—style sheets are used in math and the physical sciences. In Chapter 10, I have included a wide variety of bibliographic entries using both MLA and APA guidelines.

Because most students rely heavily on books, magazine articles, and newspaper articles for research, I'll give you the rules for those materials here.

Bibliography listings typically include three categories of information: the author's name, the title of the work, and the publishing information. However, there are many little pieces of data that fall within those three categories. Include on your card the following information, in the following order:

For a Book:

1. Name(s) of the author(s).
2. Title of the part of the book used (if the entire book does not deal with your subject) in quotes.
3. Title of the book, underlined.
4. Name of the editor, translator, or compiler.
5. Edition used, if more than one edition has been published. (If you don't see any information about an edition, assume it's the first.)
6. Number of volume(s) used, if more than one.
7. Name of the series, if the book is part of one.
8. Place of publication, name of the publisher, and date of publication.
9. If pertinent information appears in only a small portion of the book, the page numbers on which it appears.
10. Supplementary information—any other details needed to identify the exact book you used (e.g., "Spanish language translation").

For an Article in a Magazine or Newspaper:

1. Name(s) of the author(s).
2. Title of the article in quotation marks.

3. Name of the periodical, underlined. (If you are working with a newspaper that is not widely known or nationally published, add the name of the city or town in which it is published. For example: *The Herald* [Lawrence, NJ]).
4. Series number or name, if one is given.
5. Volume number. Include this only if you are working with a scholarly journal. If you're not sure whether a periodical is considered a "scholarly journal," include the volume number just in case.
6. Date of publication. Include the edition of a newspaper, if there's more than one—i.e., morning or evening edition, early or late edition.
7. The page numbers on which the article appears. Include the section letter or number for a newspaper: A8, B12, and so on.

Of course, not every bibliography card will include all of these details. Some books may not have an editor, for example. You don't need to write "no editor" on the card; simply move on to the next applicable piece of information.

Step #2: Fill out Your Note Cards

Once your first bibliography card is finished, set it aside. Get out some blank index cards and start taking notes from your reference source. Follow these guidelines:

○ **Write one thought, idea, quote, or fact on each card...and *only* one**. If you encounter a very long quote or string of data, you can write on both the front and back of a card, if necessary. *But never carry over a note to a second card.*

What if you *can't* fit the piece of information on one card? Break it into two or more smaller pieces, then put each on a separate card.

- **Write in your own words.** Summarize key points about a paragraph or section or restate the material in your own words. Avoid copying things word for word.

- **Put quotation marks around any material copied verbatim**. It's okay to include in your paper a sentence or paragraph written by someone else to emphasize a particular point (providing you do so on a limited basis). But you must copy such statements exactly as written in the original—every word, every comma, every period. You also must always put such direct quotes within quotation marks in your paper and credit the author.

Add Organizational Details

As you finish each note card, do the following:

- **In the upper left-hand corner of the card**, write down the resource number of the corresponding bibliography card (from its left-hand corner). This will remind you where you got the information.

- **Below the resource number**, write the page number(s) on which the information appeared.

- **Get out your preliminary outline**. Under which outline topic heading does the information on your card seem to fit? Under your "I" heading? Under "III"? Jot the appropriate topic numeral in the upper right-hand corner of your note card.

  If you're not sure where the information fits into your outline, put an asterisk (*) instead of a topic numeral. Later, when you do a more detailed outline, you can try to fit these "miscellaneous" note cards into specific areas.

○ **Next to the topic numeral**, jot down a one- or two-word "headline" that describes the information on the card.

○ **When you have finished taking notes from a particular resource**, put a check mark on the bibliography card. This will let you know that you're done with that resource, at least for now.

Be sure that you transfer information accurately to your note cards.

Double check names, dates, and other statistics.

As with your bibliography cards, it's not vital that you put each of these elements in the exact places I've outlined above. You just need to be consistent: Always put the page number in the same place, in the same manner. Ditto with the resource number, the topic heading, and the headline.

Here's a sample of a completed note card to which you can refer.

Sample Completed Note Card

22	II
p. 55	unemployment/compliance

Two-thirds of all working-age disabled people are still unemployed—the same portion that was jobless when the law was passed.

Add Your Personal Notes

Throughout your note-taking process, you may want to create some "personal" note cards—your own thoughts, ideas, or impressions about your subject or your thesis.

Perhaps you've thought of a great introduction for your paper. Put it on a card. Or maybe you've thought of a personal experience that relates to your topic. Put it on a card.

Write each thought on a separate note card, just as you did information taken from other resources. Assign your note card a topic heading and mini-headline, too. In the space where you would normally put the number of the resource, put your own initials or some other symbol. (I use "M" for "My Thought.") This will remind *you* that you were the source of the information or thought.

THROW AWAY UNPROFITABLE LEADS

If a particular resource doesn't yield any useful information, take the bibliography card for it out of your stack. Stick it away in your card file, just in case you want it later.

If you're *certain* you will never want to refer back to the resource, throw the bibliography card away altogether. Then scratch the listing from your working bibliography. Don't waste precious time renumbering your remaining cards—it doesn't matter if a number is missing.

WHY ARE YOU DOING ALL THIS?

Of all the tips you'll learn in this book, this note-taking system is undoubtedly one of the most valuable. In fact, many *professional* writers swear by it (including me).

When you go to write your final bibliography, you'll have all the information you need on your bibliography cards. Just put your cards in the order that they will appear in your bibliography and copy the information.

But the biggest benefit of the system is that it helps you organize your findings and makes your writing job easier.

You'll find out *how* easy in the next chapter.

CHAPTER

SIX

Organizing Your Research

"ORDER AND SIMPLIFICATION ARE THE FIRST STEPS TOWARD THE MASTERY OF A SUBJECT."
—THOMAS MANN

Your research is done.

Which means, if you managed your time as I suggested earlier, that at least one-half of your paper—perhaps as much as three-quarters of it—is done, even though you've yet to write one word of the first draft. (And you'll soon find you have done that already, too!)

You've finished going through all of those reference materials listed in your working bibliography. You've completed your bibliography cards. You've uncovered a lot of information about your subject. And you've taken extensive notes. It's time to organize your data.

You need to decide if your temporary thesis is still on target, determine how you will organize your paper, and create a detailed outline.

QUEEN MARGARET UNIVERSITY COLLEGE LIBRARY

REVIEW YOUR THESIS STATEMENT

Take a close look at your temporary thesis statement. Does it still make sense, given all the information your research has revealed? If it doesn't, revise it.

Your research should have led you to *some* conclusion about your subject. This, in turn, should lead you to the final thesis of your paper.

SORT YOUR NOTE CARDS

Once you have your final thesis, begin thinking about how you will organize your paper. This is where the note-card system you learned in Chapter 5 really pays off. Get out all of your note cards, then:

- Group together all of the cards that share the same outline topic numeral (in the upper right-hand corner of each card).
- Put those different groups in order, according to your temporary outline—topic "I" cards on top, followed by topic "II" cards, then topic "III" cards.
- Within each topic group, sort the cards further. Put together all of the cards that share the same "headline"—the two-word title in the upper right-hand corner.
- Go through your miscellaneous topic cards—those marked with an asterisk. Can you fit any of them into your existing topic groups? If so, replace the asterisk with the topic numeral. If not, put the card at the very back of your stack.

DECIDE ON THE ORDER OF YOUR PAPER

Your note cards now should be organized according to your preliminary outline. Take a few minutes to read through your note cards, beginning at the front of the stack and moving through to the back. What you are reading is a rough sketch of your paper—the information you collected in the order you (temporarily) plan to present it.

Now, consider: Does that order still make sense? Or would another arrangement work better? For example, perhaps you had planned to use chronological order—to tell readers what happened, in the order that it happened. After reviewing your note cards, you may decide that it would be better to take a cause/effect approach—to discuss, one by one, a series of different events and explain the impact of each.

Here are some of the different organizational approaches you might consider for your paper:

1. **Chronological**. Discusses events in the order in which they happened (by time of occurrence).

2. **Spatial**. Presents information in geographical or physical order (from north to south, top to bottom, left to right, inside to outside, and so forth).

3. **Numerical/Alphabetical**. An obvious way to organize a paper on "The Ten Commandments" or "The Three Men I Admire Most," for example.

4. **Major division**. For topics that logically divide into obvious parts.

5. **How to...**grow an orchid, write a better paper, etc. Like this book, organizes material from "what to do first" to "what to do last."

6. **Problem/solution** (aka cause/effect). Presents a series of problems and possible solutions, why something happened, or predicts what *might* happen as a result of a particular cause.

7. **Effect/cause**. Discusses a condition, problem, or effect and works *backward* to what might have caused it.

8. **Compare/contrast**. Discusses similarities and differences between people, things, or events. May also be used when you want to discuss advantages and disadvantages of a method, experiment, treatment, approach, etc.

9. **Order of importance**. Discusses the most important aspects of an issue first and continues through to the least important, or vice versa. (A slight variation of this is organizing your paper from the *known* to the *unknown*.)

10. **Pro/con**. Arguments for and against a position, question, decision, approach, method, etc.

The first four sequences are considered "natural," in that the organization is virtually demanded by the subject. "A Day in the Life of…" would probably begin at dawn and end at midnight. A paper on "The Physical Destruction of 9/11" that was organized spatially could begin at Ground Zero and continue, in ever-increasing geographical circles, to describe the damage. A lab report, which would include sections on materials and equipment, procedures, and results and conclusions, is a good example of a paper organized by major division.

The other sequences are "logical," in that the order is chosen and imposed by *you,* the writer. If you're writing about an environmental issue, you might utilize the problem/solution sequence: Looser environmental laws resulted in more air pollution, which led to greater incidences of respiratory diseases, which led to higher death rates among children and seniors.... The effect/cause sequence starts with the effect and then examines the causes: Higher death rates among the young and old in a particular area are a result of a concentration of manufacturers releasing large quantities of pollutants into the water supply.

If you were doing a paper on the development of new training techniques for elite runners, you could start by discussing the most effective new technique(s) and end with the least effective (organizing your paper by *decreasing importance*), or start with the least effective and work your way to the most revolutionary (*increasing importance*).

The *general-to-specific* starts with a wide-ranging statement (the "big picture") and adds more and more detail to explain it, amplify it, or justify it. The *specific-to-general* begins with facts (specifics) and uses them to reach a larger conclusion.

Finally, a *pro/con* organization is useful when you intend to present both sides of a controversial idea or subject without necessarily supporting one or the other ("The arguments for and against the legalization of drugs").

Note that in many cases the actual order you choose is also reversible—you can move forward or backward in time, consider cause and effect or effect and cause, etc. So you actually have a dozen and a half potential ways to organize your material!

Your subject and thesis may determine which organizational approach will work best. If you have a choice of more than one, use the one with which you're most comfortable or that you feel will be easiest for you to write. (Nobody says you *have* to choose the hardest way!) Keep in mind that you can use a *blend* of two approaches. For example, you might mention events in chronological order and then discuss the cause/effect of each.

REARRANGE YOUR CARDS

If necessary, revise your general outline according to the organizational decision you just made. However, *don't* change the numerals that you have assigned to the topics in your outline. If you decide to put topic "II" first in your new outline, for example, keep using the numeral "II" in front of it. Otherwise, the topic numerals on your note cards won't match those on your outline.

If you revised your outline, reorder your note cards so that they fall in the same order as your new outline.

Now, go through each group of cards that share the same topic numeral. Rearrange them so that they, too, follow the organizational pattern you chose.

Let's presume we have taken notes for our paper on the scandals that plagued President Grant. Here's the general outline we constructed in Chapter 2:

    I.   Black Friday.

    II.   Credit Mobilier affair.

   III. The Whiskey Ring.

   IV. The Belknap bribery.

    V.   Effect of scandals on Grant's presidency.

   VI. Comparison with future presidential scandals.

What should you do with all the note cards you've written? Start by sorting them into seven piles—one for each major section of your paper and one for the cards marked with an asterisk or your symbol for "my thought." Then sort the cards in the first six piles according to the headline on each card.

After you sort all of the cards that have been assigned a specific topic heading, review the remaining pile. Try to place those cards in your topic-assigned stacks.

Don't force a note card in where it does not belong. If there doesn't seem to be any logical place for the information on the card, it may be that the data just isn't relevant to your thesis. Set the card aside in a "leftover" pile. You can try again later.

And while you're setting aside inappropriate notes, don't forget to seek out "holes" in your paper—those areas that cry out for a more up-to-date fact, a good example, or a stronger transition. No one likes to discover the need to do a little more research, but if *you've* identified the omission, I guarantee your teacher will notice it. Don't let a "black hole" turn a potentially great paper into one that's merely OK just because you don't want to spend another hour online or in the library.

YOUR DETAILED OUTLINE IS DONE!

Flip through your note cards from front to back. See that? You've created a detailed outline without even knowing it. The topic numerals on your note cards match the main topics of your outline. And those headlines on your note cards? They're the subtopics for your outline. We simply transferred our notecard headlines to paper—they appear on our outline in the same order as they appear in our stack of cards.

Some instructors like to approve your outline before letting you proceed with your paper. If yours does, find out the specific outline format you are to follow. You may need to use a different numbering/lettering format from the one shown in this book.

Otherwise, you can get as detailed as you like with your outline. In most cases, a two-level outline—with topic

headings plus subheadings—will suffice. Remember that
you must have a minimum of two entries at every level of
your outline.

Here's a sample detailed outline for your President
Grant paper:

Four Scandals that Rocked the Grant Presidency

I.   Black Friday.

    A.   Attempt to corner the gold market by Jay Gould and James Fisk.

    B.   Involvement of Grant's brother-in-law.

    C.   Was Grant involved?

    D.   What Grant did.

    E.   Result of Grant's actions.

        1. And comparison to the 1929 Crash.

        2. Questions about Grant's judgement.

        3. Questions about brother-in-law's influence.

II.   Credit Mobilier affair.

    A.   Details of.

    B.   And 1872 reelection.

    C.   And Congress.

III. Whiskey Ring.

    A.   Involvement of Benjamin Bristow, Treasury Secretary.

    B.   Discoveries.

    C.   Grant's initial reaction.

    D.   Involvement of Orville Babcock.

    E.   Result.

IV.   Belknap bribery.
    A.   Details of.
    B.   Relation to administration's Indian policy.
    C.   Senate impeachment threat.
V.   Effect of scandals on Grant's presidency.
    A.   Black Friday.
    B.   Credit Mobilier affair.
    C.   Whiskey Ring.
    D.   Belknap bribery.
VI.   Comparison with later presidential scandals.
    A.   Black Friday vs. Hunt's cornering of the silver market.
    B.   Legislation to thwart Congressional bribery.
    C.   Whiskey Ring and Truman's cronies.
    D.   Future Indian policy.

BY GEORGE, I THINK YOU'VE GOT IT!

If you haven't figured it out before, you should understand now why this note-card system is so valuable. If you had written all of your notes on several dozen sheets of paper, it would be quite a task to sort out information and put it in some logical order, let alone reorder it at will.

And this isn't the only stage at which having your notes on individual cards comes in handy. As you'll see in Chapter 7, the note-card system also is helpful when you tackle the next phase of your paper—writing your rough draft.

Writing
Your Rough Draft

*"I ALWAYS DO THE FIRST LINE WELL, BUT
I HAVE TROUBLE DOING THE OTHERS."*
—MOLIERE

F or some reason, this step is the hardest for most people. It's psychological, I guess—a fear that when your thoughts actually appear in black and white, there for all the world to read, you'll be judged a complete fool.

Well, you can't do a research paper without writing. And since the job has to be done, you might as well face it right now.

Using this book, you'll find this step a lot easier than your friends probably will, assuming, of course, that you have taken good notes, organized your note cards, and prepared a detailed outline.

You may not have realized it, but you've already *done* a lot of the hard work that goes into the writing stage. You have thought about how your paper will flow, you have organized your notes, and you have prepared a detailed outline. All that's left is to transfer your information and ideas from note cards to paper.

Still, as a writer, I know that this can be a scary prospect, no matter how well you've done up to now. So, in this chapter, I'll show you some tips and tricks that will make writing your rough draft a bit easier.

Because the things you will learn in this chapter and Chapter 8 work together, read both chapters before you begin to write. Then come back and actually work through the steps outlined here.

SET THE STAGE FOR GOOD WRITING

Unfortunately for party lovers, writing is a solitary activity. Good writing takes concentration and thought. And concentration and thought require quiet—and plenty of it!

Find a quiet place to work, and do what you can to make sure you won't be interrupted. Nothing's more maddening than having the perfect phrase on the tip of your brain, only to have a friend pop in and wipe it out of your mind forever.

This will not apply to all of you. Just as some of you may find it very easy to study with the radio blaring, a few of you may not need all this quiet to write, and write well. In fact, too much quiet may work against you. Do what works for you. As I've mentioned, I tend to write, study, and do a lot of other "concentration-required" tasks with the radio pounding away. I even took notes and organized my first book while watching daytime television (though writing anything of worth while watching TV is pretty much impossible).

You also need to have plenty of desk space, so you can spread out your note cards. Your work area should be well-lit, and you should have a dictionary and thesaurus close by.

(If you need even more help, get a copy of **Get Organized**—another just-revised book in my **How to Study Program**—where all of this is discussed in far more detail.)

If possible, "write" directly onto a computer so that you can add, delete, and rearrange your words easily. Don't worry if your computer software doesn't have all the latest bells and whistles—a simple word-processing program is all you really need.

DON'T PSYCH YOURSELF OUT

If you go into this thinking you're going to turn out a teacher-ready paper on your first try, you're doomed. That kind of performance pressure leads only to anxiety and frustration.

At this point, your goal is to produce a rough draft—with the emphasis on *rough*. Your first draft isn't *supposed* to be perfect. It's *supposed* to need revision.

Relax your expectations, and you'll find that your ideas will flow much more freely. You'll be surprised at the intelligent, creative thoughts that come out of that brain of yours when you're not so worried about making a mistake.

BUILD THE FOUNDATION FIRST

The essence of good writing has little to do with grammar, spelling, punctuation, and the like. The essence of good writing is good thinking.

Sure, the mechanics of writing are important. You do need to make sure that you have everything spelled just right, that your participles aren't dangling, and that your periods and commas are placed just so.

But your thoughts, ideas, and logic are the foundation of your paper, and you need to build a foundation before you worry about hanging the front door or painting the molding. So, for now, just concentrate on getting your thoughts on paper. Don't worry about using exactly the "right" word. Don't worry about getting commas in all the right places. We'll take care of all that polishing later.

DO A NOTE-CARD DRAFT

Your note cards helped you come up with a detailed outline. Now, they're going to serve you again—by helping you plot out the paragraphs and sentences of your paper.

We're going to do some more sorting and rearranging of cards. The end result will be what I call a "note-card draft." Here's what you do:

1. Your note cards should be arranged in the same order as your detailed outline. Take out all of the note cards labeled with the numeral of the first topic on your outline.

2. Out of that stack, take out all the cards marked with the same "headline" as the first subheading in your outline.

3. Look at the information on those cards and think about how the various statistics, quotes, and facts might fit together in a paragraph.

4. Rearrange those cards so they fall in the order you have determined is best for the paragraph.

BUILDING GOOD PARAGRAPHS

Each paragraph in your paper is like a mini-essay. It should have a topic sentence—a statement of the key point or fact you will discuss in the paragraph—and contain evidence to support it. You shouldn't expect your reader to believe that your topic sentence is true just because you say so; you must back up your point with hard data. This evidence can come in different forms, such as:

- ○ Quotes from experts.
- ○ Research statistics.
- ○ Examples from research or from your own experience.
- ○ Detailed descriptions or other background information.

Paragraphs are like bricks of information—stack them up, one by one, until you have built a wall of evidence. Construct each paragraph carefully, and your readers will have no choice but to agree with your final conclusion.

If paragraphs are the bricks in your wall of evidence, transitions—sentences or phrases that move the reader from one thought to another—are the mortar that holds them together. Smooth transitions help readers move effortlessly from the summary of one paragraph to the introduction of another. (The first sentence of this paragraph is an example of a transition.)

Now put it all on paper

It's time to take the plunge and turn your note-card draft into a written rough draft. Using your cards as your guide, sit down and write.

Double- or triple-space your draft—that will make it easier to edit later. After you are finished with each note card, put a check mark at the bottom.

If you decide that you won't include information from a particular card, don't throw the card away—yet. Keep it in a separate stack. You may decide to fit in that piece of information in another part of your paper or change your mind after you read your rough draft and decide to include the information where you had originally planned.

You may, however, wind up with cards that just don't fit. If you're convinced they have no place in your paper, don't attempt to shoehorn them in anyway. Put them aside. As Johnny Cochran might proclaim, "If they blow the flow, those cards must go."

IF YOU GET STUCK...

Got writer's block already? Here are a few tricks to get you unstuck:

- **Pretend you're writing to a good friend**. Just tell him or her everything you've learned about your subject and why you believe your thesis is correct.

- **Use everyday language**. Too many people get so hung up on using fancy words and phrases that they forget that their goal is to communicate. Simpler is better.

- **Just do it**. What is it about a blank computer screen or piece of paper that scares would-be writers so badly? It happens to almost everyone, and there's only one cure I know: Just type something...anything. Once you have written that first paragraph—even if it's a really bad first paragraph— your brain will start to generate spontaneous ideas.

- **Don't edit yourself!** As you write your rough draft, don't keep beating yourself up with negative thoughts, such as "This sounds really stupid" or

"I'm a terrible writer. Why can't I express that better?" Remember: Your goal is a *rough* draft—it's supposed to stink a bit.

○ **Keep moving**. If you get hung up in a particular section, don't sit there stewing over it for hours—or even for many minutes. Just write a quick note about what you plan to cover in that section, then go on to the next section.

If you can't get even that much out, skip the section altogether and come back to it later. The point is, do whatever you have to do to keep moving forward. Force yourself to make it all the way through your paper, with as few stops as possible.

FREEWRITING AND BRAINSTORMING

Focused freewriting and brainstorming are two methods used by professional writers when the waters of creativity are dammed up somewhere in their brains. While similar, there are a couple of important differences between the two methods of getting started.

In both cases, set a brief time limit (perhaps 10 or 15 minutes), summarize your main topic in a phrase or sentence to get your thoughts moving, and do not edit or even review what you have written until the time is up.

Brainstorming is writing down everything you can think of *that relates to the topic*. It does not require that you work in any sequence or that your notes be logical or even reasonable. Asking yourself questions about the topic, no matter how strange, may help you generate new ideas.

In focused freewriting, the emphasis is on writing...*anything*...without worrying about whether what you put down is even vaguely related to your topic. The key is just to start writing—a diary entry, the biography of your dog, your thoughts about current rock videos—and *not to stop* until the time is up.

Brainstorming is useful when you are ready to write but just can't get a handle on exactly where to begin. Freewriting is useful when you can't get your brain to work at all. Both methods will help you start writing, which is all you are trying to do.

THE TROUBLE WITH PLAGIARISM

It's so tempting. You're having trouble with a sentence or section. The information you need was explained beautifully in that article you found in an old magazine. Why not just copy the section from the article? It's so musty and obscure your teacher couldn't possibly know what you've done. Why not do it?

Because plagiarism—passing off another person's words or ideas as your own—is the biggest no-no of writing research papers. It's a sure way to bring your grade down, down, down. It may earn you a failing mark. And, grades aside, you may find yourself suspended or even expelled.

"But who'll ever know that I didn't write it myself?" you wonder. Sorry, but the odds are about 999 to 1 that you will be found out. Your teachers are smarter than you think...and there's too much new software to help them nail you.

Remember, your teacher probably has been reading research papers—some of them undoubtedly on the same subject as yours—for a good many years. Those same "perfect passages" tend to pop up again and again. Do you really think your teacher will believe it's a coincidence that you wrote the exact same paragraph as that student in last year's class? That student who flunked, by the way.

Also, your teacher is familiar with your work and your writing style. That "borrowed" paragraph, written in someone else's style, is going to be noticeably different from your own prose.

Then, of course, there is the moral issue involved—but I won't get into that. You learned that stealing was wrong in kindergarten. The principle applies to written words and ideas, too.

Be especially careful of Internet sources. Far too many students seem to think if they found it on the Web, it's free to copy. The plagiarism issue aside, there are probably copyright issues involved in extensively quoting from a Web source.

How to Avoid It

To avoid plagiarism, you must give proper credit to the original author of material you use. You must also give credit for any facts, figures, or research data that you use. You do this through a *source note*—a footnote, endnote, or parenthetical note.

Sometimes, you might want to include a sentence or entire paragraph exactly as it was written by another author. If you do this, you must enclose the material in quotation marks and copy the material word for word, comma for comma. You must also offset the paragraph from the rest of the paper by indenting it from both margins, like this:

> "The author's paragraph you're quoting word for word is set off from the rest of the section by indenting it from both margins. It is also enclosed in quotation marks."

You should use this device sparingly, and only if the segment is so eloquently written or so meaningful that it makes a special impact on the reader.

You should not do this to fill up your paper the "easy" way—if your teacher is anything like most of mine were, he won't buy 7 pages of quotes in a 10-page paper.

We'll talk about how to write source notes in the next chapter. Because it's easiest to note which statements or sentences need documenting as you prepare your rough draft, go ahead and read Chapter 8 now.

But that's your only excuse for stopping or delaying your writing! As soon as you've learned the specifics about source notes, sit right down and finish your rough draft. If you keep in mind everything we've talked about in this chapter, writing your draft will be easier than you think.

I promise!

CHAPTER EIGHT

Documenting Your Sources

● ● ●

Y ou must give credit to the source of any fact, expression, or idea you use in your paper that is not your own.

For many years, the preferred way to credit (or document) sources was the footnote. Two other forms of documentation, endnotes and parenthetical notes, are popular now as well. For convenience, I'll refer to all of these different forms collectively as "source notes."

WHOSE RULES ARE THEY, ANYWAY?

In an earlier chapter, we discussed the fact that different authorities have set out different rules for bibliography listings. The same is true for source notes. Ask your instructor whose rules you are to follow.

If your teacher doesn't have a preference, you can use the method that seems easiest to you. Use the same method consistently throughout your paper—don't use a footnote on one page and an endnote on another.

I'm going to give you the MLA rules for three basic types of materials: a book, a magazine article, and a newspaper article. You can consult the *MLA Handbook for Writers of Research Papers* or other reference books if you want specific examples of how to prepare notes for more complicated types of material.

A REMINDER OF WHAT NEEDS DOCUMENTATION

You need a source note when you put any of the following in your paper:

- Quotations taken from a published source.
- Someone else's theories or ideas.
- Someone else's sentences, phrases, or special expressions.
- Facts, figures, and research data compiled by someone else.
- Graphs, pictures, and charts designed by someone else.

There are some exceptions: You don't need to document the source of a fact, theory, or expression that is common knowledge. And you don't need a source note when you use a phrase or expression for which there is no known author.

For example, if you mention that Paris is the capital of France, you don't need to document the source of that information. Ditto for time-worn phrases such as "When in Rome, do as the Romans do" or "A stitch in time, saves nine."

For a test of whether a statement needs a source note, ask yourself whether readers would otherwise think that you had come up with the information or idea all by yourself. If the answer is "yes," you need a source note. If you're in doubt, include a source note anyway.

FOOTNOTES

A footnote is a source note that appears at the "foot" (bottom) of a page of text. The footnote system works like this: You put a raised (superscript) number at the end of the statement or fact you need to document. This serves as a "flag" to readers—it tells them to look at the bottom of the page for a note about the source of the data.

In front of that footnote, you put the same superscript number as you put next to the statement or fact in your text. This tells the reader which footnote applies to which statement or fact of text.

There is no limit to the number of footnotes you may have in your paper. Number each footnote consecutively, starting with the number 1. For every footnote "flag" in your paper, be sure there is a corresponding source note at the bottom of the page.

What Goes into a Footnote

You put the same information in your footnote as you do in your bibliography listing, with two differences: In a footnote, the author's name is shown in normal order (i.e., first name first, followed by middle name or initial and last name) and the exact page number on which the information being documented appeared in the source is cited.

Most of the information for your footnotes will come from your bibliography cards, but you'll have to look at your note cards to get the actual page number from which various facts came. Arrange elements as follows:

1. Name of the author(s), first name first.
2. Title of the book or article.
3. Publication information—place of publication, name of the publisher, date of publication, and so on.
4. The number(s) of the page(s) on which the information appeared in the work.

As with bibliography listings, the content of a footnote depends on the type of reference material. For a refresher on the specific information that you need to include and in what order, see the lists in Chapter 10.

Typing Your Footnotes

The following general rules apply to all footnotes:

- Put footnotes four lines below the last line of text on the page.
- Indent the first line of a footnote five spaces.
- Single-space lines within an individual footnote; double-space between footnotes.
- Always put the superscript (raised) number of the footnote after the punctuation in your text.
- Abbreviate all months except May, June, July.

Punctuation Guidelines for Footnotes

There are specific rules of punctuation and style to follow when you write your footnotes:

For a Book:

1. Number of the note (superscript).
2. Author's first name, middle name or initial (if any), last name (comma).
3. Title of the book (underlined); no period after the title.
4. In parentheses—place of publication (colon); name of the publisher (comma); year of publication.
5. Exact page(s) on which the information you're documenting appears (period). Do not write "page" or "pg." or "p."—just the number.

For a Magazine Article:

1. Number of the note (superscript).
2. Author's first name, middle name or initial (if any), last name (comma).
3. In quotation marks—title of the article (comma).
4. Name of the periodical in which the article appeared (underlined).
5. Day the periodical was published (for a weekly or biweekly periodical); month; year (colon).
6. Exact page number(s) from which the information was taken (period).

For a Newspaper Article:

1. Number of the note (superscript).
2. Author's first name, middle name or initial (if any), last name (comma).

3. In quotation marks—title of the article (comma).

4. Name of the newspaper in which the article appeared (underlined).

5. Name of the city and town in which the paper is published (if not part of the name of the paper and/or if the paper is not widely known)—enclose in brackets and do *not* underline.

6. Day the paper was published; month; year (comma).

7. Edition (abbreviate as "ed.") if more than one is published per day (colon).

8. Section and exact page from which the information was taken (period).

If there is other information on your card—e.g., the name of an editor or series—you need to include it in your footnote. Arrange information in the same order you would for a bibliography listing. (See Chapter 10 for the order.)

Second References

The second time you cite a particular reference as a source of information, you use an abbreviated form of the footnote—just the author's last name and the page number on which the information appeared. (See sample footnote #4 below.)

If you have taken information from two different books written by the same author, you need to include the title of the book as well. If there is no author provided for the work, give the title and the page number.

Sample Footnotes

Below is a sample excerpt from a paper on the Americans with Disabilities Act, followed by four sample footnotes—three to show the different styles necessary for various sources (book, magazine article, and newspaper article), the fourth to illustrate how to cite a source for the second time:

> Two of the ADA's clauses seem to work against each other rather than with each other, and this has created problems for businesses. The law requires "reasonable accommodation" for the disabled, while, at the same time, it acknowledges that "undue hardship" is unnecessary.[1] These conflicting clauses have made interpretation frustrating for businesses and companies at every level.
>
> It seems that no industry is safe from scrutiny when it comes to compliance with the ADA.[2] The U.S. Justice Department brought a suit against Days Inns of America, saying that the company is not requiring its motels to meet the safety and access requirements of the ADA. After investigating 28 new Days Inns in 17 states over 18 months, the Justice Department found that all failed to comply with ADA regulations.[3]
>
> It's not just at the national level where there are unresolved issues. A city manager in Des Plaines, Iowa, for example, notes that local governments meet resistance when taxes need to be raised to spend money that benefits just a few members of the community.[4]

---

[1] Jill Smolowe, "Noble Aims, Mixed Results," *Time* 31 July 2003: 54.

[2] Bob Miller, *The ADA and Your Company* (New York: Fry Press, 1999) 97.

[3] Betsy Wade, "Practical Traveler: Disabled Access to Inns at Issue," *The New York Times* 14 April 2004, section 5, page 4.

[4] Smolowe 54.

ENDNOTES

Endnotes are basically the same as footnotes. Within the body of your paper, you indicate the existence of an endnote in the same manner as you would for a footnote—with a superscript (raised) number. The only difference is that you put all of your source listings on a separate page at the end of the text, instead of at the bottom of each page.

Title the last page of your paper "Notes" and center that title at the top of the page. Leave a one-inch margin on all sides of the paper (top, bottom, left, and right).

List endnotes consecutively (put endnote 1 first, then note 2, and so forth.). As with your footnotes, indent the first line of each note. Double space the entire page (both within individual notes and between notes). Follow the same punctuation rules as those given for footnotes.

PARENTHETICAL NOTES

Parenthetical notes are probably the easiest way to document sources. In this system, you put a brief source note right in the body of your text, enclosed in parentheses (hence the name "parenthetical notes").

Generally, your reference includes only the last name of the author and the page number from which the information was taken. For example:

Two thirds of all working-age disabled people are still unemployed. This is the same portion that was jobless when the law was passed (Smolowe 55).

To find complete details about the source, readers refer to your bibliography. In this case, they would look for a book or article by "(Somebody) Smolowe."

Make sure your note includes enough information so your readers will know exactly which source in your bibliography you are citing. For example, if your bibliography lists two different works, both written by authors with the last name of Smolowe, you should include the author's first name in your parenthetical note, i.e., (Jill Smolowe 55).

If you have two books, articles, or whatever written by the same author, include the title of the book you are citing. You can use an abbreviation of the title, if you want. In this case, you might say (Smolowe, Noble Aims 55).

If your source is a one-page article, you don't have to give any page number in your note.

NOW OR LATER?

You can incorporate your source notes as you write your rough draft, or you can put them in during a later draft. I suggest you do the following:

1. As you write your rough draft, mark any statement of fact that needs to be documented. Note the number of the source (the number in the upper left-hand corner of your note card) and the page number from which the material was taken. For example: "Two thirds of all working-age disabled people are still unemployed—the same portion that was jobless when the law was passed. (#2-55)."

2. As you prepare your final draft, simply convert these "preliminary" notes into your formal ones.

3. Continue on through the rest of your text, consecutively numbering each note.

4. If you are using footnotes or endnotes: When you come to the first "preliminary" note in your text,

replace the source number and page number code with the superscript numeral "1." Find the bibliography card with the same source number as that in your preliminary note. Type your footnote or endnote using the data from the bibliography card. Use the same page number that you show in your "preliminary" note.

5. If you are using parenthetical notes: Find the bibliography card that matches the source number in your preliminary note. Replace the source number/page number code with your parenthetical note. Again, you already know which page number to cite, since you had that information in your preliminary note.

Revising
Your Masterpiece

Y ou can breathe a big sigh of relief—your rough
draft is done!

Now you need to take that rough-cut diamond and polish it into a sparkling gem. In the remaining chapters of this book, we'll revise your rough cut—and revise it again—until we arrive at your final draft.

As we've done with other parts of your assignment, we'll break this process into several steps.

In this chapter, we'll work through two of those steps. First, you'll edit your paper for content and clarity. Then you'll work on the finer points—grammar, spelling, sentence construction, and so forth.

PHASE 1: EDIT FOR MEANING

As I said, we're not going to handle all your revisions in one pass. At this point, you still don't need to concentrate on grammar, spelling, and other technical aspects of your paper. Of course, when you notice flaws in these areas, fix them, but don't get hung up on them right now.

Rather, during *this* phase of the revision process, you should be trying to:

- **Improve** the flow of your paper—from paragraph to paragraph, sentence to sentence.
- **Organize** your thoughts and information better.
- **Clarify** any confusing points.
- **Strengthen** any weak arguments—by explaining your argument better or adding more data to support your point of view.

Revision Checklist

As you review your rough draft, ask yourself the following questions:

- Do your thoughts move logically from one point to the next?
- Is the meaning of every sentence and paragraph crystal clear?
- Does every sentence make a point—or support one?
- Do you move smoothly from one paragraph to the next? Or do you jump randomly from one topic to another?
- Do you support your conclusions with solid evidence—research data, examples, statistics?

○ Do you include a good *mix* of evidence—quotes from experts, scientific data, personal experiences, historical examples?

○ Do you have a solid introduction and conclusion?

○ Did you write in your own words and style? Or have you merely strung together phrases and quotes "borrowed" from other authors?

○ Have you explained your subject thoroughly, or assumed that readers have more knowledge about it than they actually might? (Remember: *You're* familiar with the topic now, but just because something is now obvious to you doesn't mean your readers will know what you're talking about.)

○ Have you convinced your readers that your thesis is valid?

○ Is there information that, while correct and informative, just doesn't belong? Cut it out!

○ Have you maintained a consistent point of view (i.e., first, second, or third person throughout)?

○ Does your last paragraph successfully summarize the entire paper and effectively "close" your argument?

Mark any trouble spots with a colored pencil or pen. If you have an idea on how to fix a section, jot it down on your rough draft.

Then ask a friend or parent to read your paper. Ask them which sections were confusing, which didn't seem to fit in as written. Make notes on your draft about these trouble points.

Now sit down and begin to rewrite. Focus on all of those problem areas you found. If necessary, add new information. Play with sentences, paragraphs, even entire sections.

If you're working with a computer, this is fairly easy to do. You can flip words, cut and add sentences, and rearrange whole pages with a few keystrokes.

If you're still hunched over a typewriter or scratching along with pen and paper, you can do the same thing using scissors and tape. Just cut up the pages of your rough draft and tape them together in their new order.

If you can't figure out how to fix a bothersome sentence or paragraph, take some time out from writing. Think about what it is you're trying to tell the reader—what point are you trying to get across?

Once you get your thoughts straight, the words will usually take care of themselves.

REWORK YOUR OPENING AND CLOSING PARAGRAPHS

When you feel you have created a wonderful paper, examine your opening and closing paragraphs. Take the time to go over these—again and again—to make them the best you possibly can. More than one "okay-not-great" paper has earned a better-than-expected grade because of an "A+" introduction and conclusion.

Your paper's opening paragraph is the most important of all. It sets out what you will be arguing for or against (and why you chose that side) and introduces the rest of the paper. If it's well written, it will seamlessly lead your teacher into the rest of the paper and earn you points for solid organization. If it's poorly written, it may not matter what follows—your teacher may conclude you obviously don't know what you're talking about and grade accordingly (*while spending less time than he might have otherwise on the rest of the paper*).

Think of the introduction and the conclusion as the bread in a sandwich, with the information in between as the hamburger, lettuce, tomato, and pickle. The main attraction may be what's between the slices, but you need the bread to even call it a sandwich.

Here are some ways to start off your paper with a little zing:

- Say something that grabs attention.
- Say something controversial.
- Paint a picture of a scene.
- Recreate an event.
- Use a potent quote.
- Ask a provocative question.

But don't—absolutely do *not*—use a joke. The joke will be on you. Most teachers have no sense of humor once they start grading papers (presuming they did before).

PHASE 2: DO THE DETAIL WORK

When you finish editing for content and meaning, print a clean copy of your paper.

It's time to double check all of your facts for accuracy and deal with those things I've been telling you to delay on: sentence structure, grammar, punctuation, spelling, and so on.

Comb through your paper and check every piece of factual information against your note cards:

- Did you spell names, terms, and places correctly?
- When you quoted dates and statistics, did you get your numbers straight?

○ Do you have a source note (or preliminary source note) for every fact, expression, or idea that is not your own?

○ If you quoted material from a source, did you quote that source exactly? Did you put the material in quotation marks?

Mark any corrections on your new draft. Again, use a colored pen or pencil so you can easily spot corrections later.

Smooth out the Edges

You've already fixed major problem areas in your paper. Now take an even closer look at your sentences and paragraphs. Try to make them smoother, tighter, and easier to understand.

○ Use action verbs and the active voice: "Some apes in captivity have survived for 30 or more years" is better than "Ages of 30 years or more have been enjoyed by some apes in captivity."

○ Consider dropping constructions beginning with "there is (was)" from your vocabulary: "There was a storm at sea" is a tired and boring way to proclaim, "A storm raged."

○ Is there too much fat? Seize every opportunity to make the same point in fewer words.

○ Are there places where phrasing or construction is awkward? Try to rearrange the sentence or section so that it flows better.

○ Did you use descriptive, colorful words? Did you tell your reader, "The planes were damaged," or paint a more colorful and creative picture: "The planes were broken-down hulks of rusted metal— bullet-ridden, neglected warbirds that could barely limp down the runway."

○ Consult a thesaurus for synonyms that work better than the words you originally chose. But don't get carried away and use words so obscure that the average reader wouldn't know their meaning. When in doubt, opt for the familiar word rather than the obscure, the shorter vs. the longer, the tangible vs. the hypothetical, the direct word vs. the roundabout phrase.

○ Have you overused cliches or slang expressions? Especially in academic writing, neither are particularly appreciated. Your paper may be "dead as a doornail" if you don't "get the lead out," get rid of some of the "oldies but goodies," and make sure your paper is "neat as a pin."

○ Have you overused particular words? Constantly using the same words makes your writing boring. Check a thesaurus for other possibilities.

○ How do the words *sound?* When you read your paper aloud, does it flow like a rhythmic piece of music? Or plod along like a funeral dirge?

○ One of the best ways to give your writing a little "oomph" is to vary your sentence structure. Use short sentences occasionally. Even very short. Without subjects. Use simple sentences, complex sentences (an independent clause and one or more dependent clauses), and embedded sentences (combining two clauses using relative pronouns rather than conjunctions). And despite what Mrs. Dougherty taught you in eighth grade, it really is okay to start sentences with "and" or "but." And to use sentence fragments for emphasis and effect. Really.

○ Always remember the point of the paper: to communicate your ideas as clearly and concisely as possible. So don't get lost in the details. If you have to choose between that "perfect" word and the most organized paper imaginable, opt for the latter.

Again, mark corrections on your draft with a colored pen or pencil. No need to retype your paper yet—unless it's gotten so marked up that it's hard to read!

Check Your Grammar and Spelling

Here's the part that almost nobody enjoys. It's time to rid your paper of mistakes in grammar and spelling.

I know that I've told you all along that your thoughts are the most important element of your paper. It's true. But it's also true that glaring mistakes in grammar and spelling will lead your teacher to believe that you are either careless or downright ignorant—neither of which will bode well for your final grade.

So, get out your dictionary and a reference book on English usage and grammar. If you don't happen to own the latter, check one out from the library, or better yet, buy one. (This won't be the last time you'll use it, so it's a good investment.) Ask your instructor to recommend a few good choices.

Scour through your paper, sentence by sentence, marking corrections with your colored pen or pencil. Ferret out:

○ **Misspelled words.** Check every word. Ask yourself: "If I had to bet $100 that I spelled that word correctly, would I pull out my wallet?" No? Then you'd better look it up in the dictionary! Watch out especially for words your spell-check program may not catch, such as "too" instead of "to" or "your" instead of "you're."

○ **Incorrect punctuation.** Review the rules regarding placement of commas, quotation marks,periods, and other punctuation. Make sure you follow those rules throughout your paper.

○ **Incorrect sentence structure.** Look for dangling participles, split infinitives, sentences that end in prepositions, and other no-no's.

Again, review the rules about such matters in your reference book.

PHASE 3: PREPARE THE ALMOST-FINAL DRAFT

Retype your paper, making all those corrections you marked as you completed Phase 2. As you prepare this draft of your paper, incorporate the following three steps:

1. Format the paper according to your teacher's instructions—use the specified page length, margins, and line spacing. If you haven't been given any instructions in this area, follow these guidelines:

   ○ Type or print on one side of the paper only.
   ○ Use 8-1/2 x 11 paper.
   ○ Leave a one-inch margin all around—top, bottom, right, and left.
   ○ Indent the first word of each paragraph five spaces from the left margin.
   ○ Double space all text. (Single space footnotes, but double space between each.)
   ○ Number your pages in the upper right-hand corner of the paper, one-half inch from the top.

2. Incorporate your final footnotes, endnotes, or parenthetical notes. For specifics on how to do this, refer back to Chapter 8.

3. Give your paper a title, if you haven't already done so. Your title should be as short and sweet as possible, but it should tell readers what they can expect to learn from your paper. Don't get cute or coy—that's for magazine covers (and it's pretty annoying even then).

Some teachers prefer that you put your title, name, date, and class number on a separate title page. Others want this information to appear at the top of the first page of your text. As always, ask your instructor which format to follow.

Now, give yourself a big pat on the back! The toughest parts of your assignment are all behind you.

CHAPTER

TEN

Compiling Your Final Bibliography

B y the time you've completed the revision process outlined in Chapter 9, your paper should be in very good shape. Give yourself a round of applause!

You still need to prepare your final bibliography, which I'll show you how to do in this chapter. Lastly, you'll need to proofread your paper and type your final draft. Those steps are covered in Chapter 11.

"WORKS CONSULTED" VS. "WORKS CITED"

Your teacher may ask for a *"works consulted"* bibliography, a list of all reference materials you reviewed during your research, *even if nothing from them was incorporated in your paper*. Or you may be asked to do a *"works cited"* bibliography, listing only the materials you mentioned in the footnotes, endnotes, or parenthetical notes.

If your teacher does not specify which type of bibliography to include, choose the first. It will be a better indication of the range of research you've done.

There are some very specific technical rules you must follow when preparing your bibliography. These rules are the same whether you are doing a "works consulted" or "works cited" bibliography.

Your bibliography listings contain virtually the same information as footnotes or endnotes. But as we've already learned, there are two big variations: (1) The format and punctuation are different, and (2) the page number references are different.

Somewhere along the line, people made up these rules. I'm sure there were good reasons for the things they decided, but the reasons aren't important. What *is* important is that you follow the rules—like them or not.

Remember, different authorities prefer different rules, so check with your teacher or professor to find out which rules he or she prefers you follow. I've included detailed examples using both MLA and APA guidelines.

LAYING OUT YOUR BIBLIOGRAPHY PAGE

Your bibliography should be at the end of your paper, on a separate page or pages:

- One inch from the top of the page: Center the title "Works Cited" or "Works Consulted," depending upon which type of bibliography you're doing.
- Use the same margins as you did for the rest of your paper—one inch all the way around.

○ Treat your bibliography pages as if they are a continuation of the text of your paper and number them accordingly—don't start repaginating.

○ List sources alphabetically by the author's last name. If no author is given, list by the first word in the title of the work (unless the first word is "A," "An," or "The," in which case list by the second word of the title).

○ The first line of each listing should be flush with the left margin. Indent all other lines five spaces from the left margin.

○ Double space all listings and double space between entries.

○ Abbreviate all months except May, June, and July.

SORT YOUR BIBLIOGRAPHY CARDS

You will take all of the information for your bibliography directly from your bibliography cards. Before typing, put your bibliography cards in the correct alphabetical order. Then, just transfer all the information, card by card, following the examples that follow, presuming you are following either MLA or APA guidelines.

SAMPLE MLA ENTRIES

Note that you can underline titles of books, journals, magazines, newspapers, and films instead of italicizing them, as I have here. If you have any questions about MLA style, consult the sixth (2003) edition of the *MLA Handbook*.

Anthology or Collection
Pelosi, Jeffrey R., ed. *The Life and Times of Buckaroo Banzai*. New York: Printing Press, 2001.

Advertisement
Brooks, Anne. "Buy These Books!" Career Press. Advertisement. *Publishers Weekly*. 3 March 2003: 63.

A Part of a Book (e.g. Essay in a Collection)
Fried, Allen. "Rock and Roll Redux." *The Rock Anthology*. Ed. Keith Richards. London: Henry Higgins Publishers, 1999. 14–17. (14–17 are page numbers.)

Article from a Reference Book
"Sharks." *Worldwide Encyclopedia*. 2001 ed.

Article in a Scholarly Journal
Brienza, Brenda. "OCD: A New Perspective." *Journal of Innovative Psychology* 43 (2001): 522–527. ("43" is the volume; 522–527 are page numbers.)

Book
Simplex, Vernon C. *Wallace Stevens: A Life*. New York: Jodi Books, 1999.

Book or Movie Review
Kennedy, Douglas. "Whose Money is it Anywho?" Rev. of *Get Rich Slow*, by Tama McAleese. *Banking Journal* July 2003: 144–146.

CD-ROM or DVD

Grammar Essentials Library. CD-ROM. Microsoft, 2004.

Computer Database

Ryan, Thomas. "Softball Statistical Analysis." *Statistical Abstracts* 1999. Ryan Database, items 44–498.

Definition from a Dictionary

"Aboriginal." Def. 3 *Modern Australian Dictionary.* 1994.

Encyclopedia

"Wilder, Thornton." *The World Book Encyclopedia.* 1994 ed.

Essay in a Journal

LaRocca, Karen. "A New Perspective on Gilgamesh." *Medieval Genres* 32.5 (1997): 22–33. ("32" is the volume; "5" is the issue number, which must be included if each issue of a journal begins on page 1.)

Government Publication

Canada. Minister of Eskimo Affairs. *How Many Igloos?* Ottawa: Minister of Territorial Affairs Canada 2003.

Magazine Article

Rutigliano, Tony. "It Don't Get Any Better." *Pizza Today* 24 Apr. 1998: 22–28.

Movie or Film

The Godfather. Writ. Francis Ford Coppola and Mario Puzo. Dir. Francis Ford Coppola. Prod. Albert S. Ruddy. Perf. Marlon Brando, James Caan, Al Pacino. Paramount Pictures, 1972.

Musical Score

LaPlaca, Frank. *Symphony in D Major Op. 5, No.3.* New York: Buddha Music, 1999.

Newspaper Article

Kennedy, Melissa. "High Fashion at the Crossroads." *New York Newsday* 14 May 2003, late ed.: B4.

Online Encyclopedia

"Champagne." *Worldwide Encyclopedia.* 2003. 6 July 2004 http://www.worldwide enc.com/article?eu=33327.

Online Government Publication

Canada. Office of the Bureau of Mines. *Get the Lead Out.* 7 Feb. 2002. 8 July 2004 http://www.obmsct.ca/mmb/account/OBM.html.

Online Interview

Thatcher, Margaret. Interview. Prime Minister's Office. 1995. 3 March 2004 http://www.pm.gov.uk/Page 4848.asp.

Online Magazine

Kelly, Laurie. "Witchcraft on the Rise." 19 March 2003. *Witch Journal* 6 July 2004 http://www.witch.nmt.au/kelly/index.

Online Scholarly Journal

Kristoff, Edward. "A new definition of racism." *Journal of Public Affairs* 44:10 (2004). 8 July 2004 http://www.jpubaffairs.org/research/Kristoff_main.htm.

Poem

Poe, Edgar Allen. "Annabel Lee." *The Collected Works of Edgar Allen Poe*. Ed. William C. Farnsworth. New York: Columbia UP, 1972. 218–221.

Play

Wilder, Thornton. "Our Town." *Great 20th Century Playwrights*. Ed. Steven Turcotte. 8th ed. Austin: Kathleen Pr, 1998.

Radio/Television Program

"Remaking The Thin Red Line." Ramblings with Dave Field. ABC. WZRX, Boston. 22 Jan. 2004.

Short Story

Poe, Edgar Allen. "Hop Frog." *The Collected Works of Edgar Allen Poe*. Ed. William C. Farnsworth. New York: Columbia UP, 1972. 222–241.

Sample APA Entries

I have not duplicated all of the entries in the previous section, but just enough to show the clear differences between the styles. Downloadable information on APA styles is available at: http://apastyle.net

Annual Periodical

Brooks, A. (2002). I Can Sell! *Sales Power Annual*, 22, 204–220.

Article from a Reference Book

Clampett, Ellie Mae. (2003). Sharks. In the *Worldwide Encyclopedia*. (Vol. 22, pp. 200–202). Des Moines: Worldwide Press.

Article in a Scholarly Journal

Brienza, Brenda. (2001). OCD: A New Perspective. *Journal of Innovative Psychology* 43, 522–527. ("43" is the volume; 522–527 are page numbers.)

Book

Simplex, Vernon C. (1999). *Wallace Stevens: A Life*. New York: Jodi Books.

Book or Movie Review

Kennedy, D. (July 2003). Whose Money is it Anywho? (Review of the book *Get Rich Slow*). *Banking Journal*, 144–146.

Computer Software

Parcells, T. (2002). *Gaming*. (Computer software).

Edited Book

Beucler, K. (Ed.). (2000). *The art of the possible*. New York: Beucler Books.

Encyclopedia

Farkas, S. (Ed.). (2003) Dictionary of editing solutions (5th ed., Vols. 2–6). New York: Clayton Press.

Government Report

Ottawa: Minister of Territorial Affairs. (2003). *How Many Igloos?* Canada: Minister of Eskimo Affairs.

Magazine Article

Rutigliano, Tony. (1998, April 24). It Don't Get Any Better. *Pizza Today*, 22–28.

Musical Score

LaPlaca, F. (1999). *Symphony in D Major Op. 5, No.3*. New York: Buddha Music.

Newsletter Article

Kelly, Laurie. (2003, Spring). On racism. *Southern Law Center Minutes*, 44, 34–36.

Newspaper Article

Kennedy, Melissa. High Fashion at the Crossroads. (2003, May 14). *New York Newsday*, p. B4.

Online Article

Kristoff, E. (2004). Dealing with returns. *Shipping News*, 9, 27–29. Retrieved August 8, 2004, from: http://shippingnews.net/2004-9-kristoff.html.

Radio/Television Program

(2004, Jan. 22). Remaking The Thin Red Line. *Ramblings with Dave Field*. Boston: WZRX.

CHAPTER

ELEVEN

Applying Finishing Touches

Can you see it? That light at the end of the tunnel? You should—you're 99 percent of the way *through* the research paper tunnel.

Don't shut down your mental engine just yet, though—there are a couple of tricky turns left to negotiate.

First, you need to proofread your paper. Then, you need to type or print out a perfect copy of your manuscript—and proofread it again.

To be a good proofreader, you need a sharp eye. Unfortunately, your poor eyes are probably pretty tired by now. And you've become so familiar with your paper that it may be difficult for you to see it clearly. You're likely to read phrase by phrase, rather than word by word. And that means that you'll likely skip right over some typos and other errors.

In this chapter, I'll show you some tricks that will help you overcome these problems and catch all those little bugaboos in your manuscript.

READ YOUR PAPER ALOUD

Go to a quiet room, and read your paper aloud. Not in your head—actually speak the words you have written. Sound them out, syllable by syllable. You'll quickly pick up typos and misspelled words.

Circle any errors that you find with a brightly colored pen or pencil. You'll want to spot them easily and quickly when you type up your final draft.

WORK BACKWARD

This is another great trick. Read your paper from back to front, starting with the last word on the last page, working backward toward your introduction. This will help you focus on each individual word, rather than on the meaning of your phrases and sentences.

HAVE SOMEONE ELSE READ YOUR PAPER

Ask a parent, sibling, or other relative to read your paper. Or trade papers with a classmate—you'll read his if he reads yours. Someone who has never seen your paper before is much more likely to catch a mistake than someone who has read it again and again. (Just be careful about the person you pick and the instructions you give.

If you're two days away from turning in your paper, you don't want to hear from your anal-retentive friend how *he* would have organized the paper.)

Prepare your perfect copy

After you've proofread your paper several times (at *least* three times), type or print out a clean draft. Then proofread it *again*, to make sure you caught every single error. Miss one or two? Print those pages again and *proofread again*. Continue until you're sure your paper is error-free.

I have often noticed when my editors format a book that making a single correction somehow leads to a mistake elsewhere on the page. It makes absolutely no sense to me, but it seems to happen. Which is why you need to proofread your entire paper *one last time*!

Get it all together

Be sure to put your final draft on quality white paper. Don't use that erasable typing paper! It smudges easily.

If you've written your paper on a computer, avoid printing your final draft on a low-quality dot-matrix or bubble-jet printer. Manuscripts printed on such printers are sometimes hard to read—and you obviously don't want to make it difficult for your teacher to read your paper. (Some instructors do not even accept such printer copy.)

You can also save your paper on a floppy disk and take the disk to a quick-print shop. Providing you're working on a compatible computer system, the shop can print out your paper on a laser printer, which produces typeset-quality printing. If your school has a computer lab, there might be a few good quality printers available there as well.

If you don't have access to a good printer, or if you're just a lousy typist, you may want to have your final draft prepared by a professional typist or computer service bureau. Just make sure the one you select can have your paper done in plenty of time to meet your final deadline!

As soon as you complete your final draft, head right for the copy shop. Pay the buck or two it costs to make a copy of your paper. In the event that you lose or damage your original manuscript, you will have a backup copy.

Here's a great tip: Type the file name for your report right at the top of your copy. That way, if you ever have to refer back to the report, you'll know exactly where to find it on your hard drive. This is especially important if you're not using long file names and have to remember what Jdtxthis.doc stands for!

TURN IN YOUR ASSIGNMENT

Put your paper in a new manuscript binder or folder, unless your instructor asks you to do otherwise. Then, turn in your paper—on time, of course!

AND CONGRATULATE YOURSELF!

You have just completed one of the most challenging assignments you will face as a student. You should feel a real sense of accomplishment. Remember, you can use many of the same strategies you learned as we put together your research paper when you prepare essays, oral reports, and other school assignments (which, as it turns out, I'll discuss in the next chapter). And the skills you developed during the past few weeks or months will be useful to you long after you've left the classroom behind for good.

So accept my congratulations, and treat yourself to a little celebration.

Essay Tests
and Oral Reports

A pproach essay questions the same way you would a paper. While you can't check your textbook or go to the library or online to do research, the facts, ideas, comparisons, and whatever else you need are in your own cerebral library—your mind.

Don't ever, *ever* begin writing the answer to an essay question without a little "homework" first. I don't care if you're the school's prize-winning journalist.

First, really look at the question. Are you sure you know what it's asking? What are the verbs? Don't "describe" when it calls for you to "compare and contrast." Don't "explain" when it tells you to "argue." Underline the verbs. (See page 114 for a list of the most-used verbs in essay tests and what each instructs you to do.)

Then sit back a minute and think about what you're going to write. Or less than a minute, depending on how much time you have, but don't just start writing.

You need to budget your time for an essay test just as you should for any test—the mathematical calculations are just easier. Five questions in 50 minutes? Doesn't take an Einstein to figure out 10 minutes per essay.

Or does it? In this example, allow 7 or 8 minutes per essay, which will give you anywhere from 10 to 15 minutes to review, proofread, and make corrections and additions to all your answers. And if any of the questions are "weighted" more than the others, adjust the time you spend on them accordingly.

When the time you've budgeted for the first question is up, immediately move on to the next, no matter how far you've gotten on the first. You'll have time at the end—if you follow my suggestion—to go back and add more. *Most teachers will give you a better overall grade for five incomplete but decent essays than for three excellent ones and two left blank.*

Here's the step-by-step way to answer every essay question.

Step 1: On a blank sheet of paper or on the back of your test paper or blue book, write down all the facts, ideas, concepts, and so forth, you feel should be included in your answer.

Step 2: Organize them in the order in which they should appear. You don't have to rewrite your notes into a detailed outline—why not just number each note according to where you want to place it?

Step 3: Compose your first paragraph, working on it just as long and as hard as I suggested you do on your papers. It should summarize and introduce the key points you will make in your essay. *This is where superior essay answers are made or unmade.*

Step 4: Write your essay.

Step 5: Reread your essay and, if necessary, add points left out, correct spelling, grammar, and punctuation. Also watch for a careless omission that could cause serious damage—like leaving out a "not" and making the point opposite of the one you wanted to write.

If there is a particular fact you know is important and should be included but you just don't remember it, guess if you can. Otherwise, just leave it out and do the best you can. If the rest of your essay is well thought out and organized and clearly communicates all the other points that should be included, I doubt most teachers will mark you down too severely for such an omission.

Don't set yourself up for a poor grade by making guesses you really don't have to. If you think something occurred in 1804 but are afraid it could be 1805 or 1806, just write "in the first decade of the 19th century." You probably will *not* be marked down for the latter phrase, but *will* lose a point or two if you cite a wrong date.

Remember: Few teachers will be impressed by length. A well-organized, well-constructed, specific answer will always get you a better grade than "shotgunning"—writing down everything you know in the faint hope that you will actually hit something. Worry less about the specific words and more about the information. Organize your answer to a fault and write to be understood, not to impress. Better to use shorter sentences, paragraphs, and words—and be clear and concise—than to let the teacher fall into a clausal nightmare from which he may never emerge (and neither will your A!).

If you don't have the faintest clue what the question means, ask. If you still don't have any idea of the answer—

and I mean zilch—leave it blank. Writing down everything you think you know about the supposed subject in the hopes that one or two things will actually have something to do with the question is, in my mind, a waste of everyone's time. Better to allocate the time you would waste to other parts of the test and do a better job on those.

THE BEST-ORGANIZED BEATS THE BEST-WRITTEN

While I think numbering your notes is as good an organizational tool as jotting down a complete outline, there is certainly nothing wrong with fashioning a quick outline. Not one with Roman numerals—it will be a simple list of abbreviated words, scribbled on a piece of scrap paper or in the margin of your test booklet. The purpose of this outline is the same as those fancy ones: to make sure you include everything you need and want to say—in order.

No one is going to grade this outline. In fact, the only person who's even going to *see* it is your teacher, who will undoubtedly be impressed that you took a moment to organize your thoughts before rushing into the essay. I might as well make my "quality, not quantity" speech here, too. I hope you write well. It's important. But excellent writing, even pages and pages of it, will not get you an excellent grade unless you have the quality—hard-hitting, incisive, direct answers.

Again, most teachers won't fall for the beautifully crafted, empty answer. Don't depend on your good looks or your command of the subjunctive to get you by. Study.

Think of the introduction and the conclusion as the bread in a sandwich, with the information in between as the hamburger, lettuce, tomato, and pickle. All the ingredients are necessary, but the tastiest part is inside the bun.

PROOF IT!

Budget your time so that you can go back over your essay, slowly, and correct any mistakes or make any additions. Check your spelling, punctuation, grammar, and syntax. It would be a shame for you to write a beautiful essay and lose points because you had those kinds of errors.

WHEN YOU'RE DONE, YOU'RE *ALMOST* DONE

Resist the temptation to leave the room or turn in your paper before you absolutely have to. Imagine the pain of sitting in the cafeteria starting to eat your lunch, while everyone else is back in the classroom, continuing to work on the test, and you suddenly remember what else you could have said to make your essay really sparkle. But it's too late!

Make sure you can't, simply can't, add anything more to any of the essay answers before you walk out of the test.

IF YOU RUN OUT OF TIME

While you should have carefully allocated sufficient time to complete each essay before you started working on the first, things happen. You may find yourself with two minutes left and one essay to go. What do you do? As quickly as possible, write down everything you think should be included in your answer and number each point in the order in which you would have written it. If you then have time to reorganize your notes into a better-organized outline, do so. Many teachers will give you at least partial credit if your outline contains all the information the answer was supposed to. It will at least show you knew a lot about the subject and were capable of outlining a reasonable response.

One of the reasons you may have left yourself with insufficient time to answer one or more questions is because you knew too darned much about the previous question(s). And you wanted to make sure the teacher knew you knew, so you wrote…and wrote…and wrote…until you ran out of time.

Be careful—some teachers throw in a relatively general question that, if you wanted to, you could write about until next Wednesday. In that case, they aren't testing your knowledge of the whole subject as much as your ability to edit yourself, to organize and summarize the important points.

Just remember that no matter how fantastic your answer to any one essay, it is going to get one-fifth the overall score (presuming 5 questions)—that is, 20 points, never more, even if you turn in a publishable book manuscript. Meanwhile, 80 points are still up for grabs.

ORAL REPORTS

There are some key differences between writing a report and presenting it orally, especially if you don't want to make the mistake of just reading your report in front of the class.

Good notes are your lifeline when you stand up to say what's on your mind. They should act as cues to remind you where your talk should go next, and they should make you feel secure that you can get through the ordeal.

However, notes can also be a crutch that guarantees not success, but audience boredom. You've probably seen any number of people get up in front of an audience and just read some papers they have in front of them. I guarantee you that, as a relative novice at public speaking, you will make one (and maybe all) of these "Big Three" mistakes if you bring your entire text with you:

- ○ You will read from it, failing to make eye contact with your audience. This will help to ensure that you lose their interest and your credibility. How familiar can you be with a subject if you have to read your entire speech?

- ○ If you stop reading for a second to ad lib or look at your listeners, you will lose your place. It's much harder to find that key word that will jog your memory on a full page of text than on an index card.

- ○ You won't be familiar enough with your speech, because, after all, you'll have it there with you, so why bother rehearsing or memorizing anything?

Getting Ready to Get Ready

Exactly what sort of talk is this going to be? Odds are, if you've been assigned to give a talk for a class, it will fall into one of the following categories:

- ○ **Exposition:** A straightforward statement of facts.
- ○ **Argument:** Tries to change the opinions of at least a portion of the audience.
- ○ **Description:** Provides a visual picture to your listeners.
- ○ **Narration:** Storytelling.

The most common forms of oral reports assigned in school will be the exposition and argument. You'll find that you will research and organize your information for these types of speeches pretty much the way you would a term paper. So, review Chapter 8.

A note of caution: If you're preparing an *argument*, don't convince yourself you don't have to research *both* sides of the topic just because you're only presenting *one* of them. You should be doubly prepared with all the facts, as you might be challenged with questions or the arguments of other speakers.

As you gather information for your report, making notes on index cards as you did for your term paper, keep this in mind: In order for you to be effective, you must use some different techniques when you *tell* your story rather than *write* it. Here are a few:

○ **Don't make your topic too broad.** This advice, offered for preparing written reports as well, is even more important when preparing a talk. Try giving an effective speech on "Eleanor Roosevelt," "Jane Austen's novels," or "The U.S. military" in 15 minutes, frequently the amount of time assigned for oral reports. These topics are more suited to a series of books!

"How Eleanor Roosevelt changed the role of First Lady," "The way the movie *Clueless* failed to meet the standards set by Austen's *Emma*," or "The pros and cons of inoculating all military personnel with the anthrax vaccine" are more manageable topics. Narrowing the scope of your talk will help you research and organize it more effectively.

○ **Don't overuse statistics.** While they're very important for lending credibility to your position, too many will only weigh down your speech and bore your audience.

○ **Anecdotes add color and life to your talk.** But use them sparingly, because they can slow down your speech. Get to the punch line before the yawns start.

○ **Be careful with quotes.** Unlike a term paper, a speech allows you to establish yourself as an authority with less fear of being accused of plagiarism. So you can present a lot more facts without attribution. (But you'd better have the sources in case you're asked about your facts.) You can use quotes, though, when they contain distinctive language or elicit an emotion. Be sure to attribute the source.

I've found that trying to shuffle a bunch of papers in front of a class is difficult. Note cards that fit in the palm of your hand are a lot easier to use, but only if the notes on them are very short and to the point. Then they act as "triggers" rather than verbatim cue cards—hanging on to 300 note cards is as difficult as a sheaf of papers.

Remember: You'll actually be holding these cards in your sweaty palms and speaking from them, so write *notes*, not whole sentences. The shorter the notes—and the more often you practice your report so each note triggers the right information—the more effective your report will be. (And the less you will have to look at them, making eye contact with your class and teacher easier.)

Here are some other ways to make your oral reports more effective:

○ Pick out one person to talk to—preferably a friend, but any animated and/or interested person will do—and direct your talk at him or her.

○ Practice, *practice*, **practice** your presentation. Jangled nerves are often the result of a lack of confidence. The more confident you are that you know your material, the less nervous you will be, and the better and more spontaneous your presentation will be.

○ If you are like me and suffer from involuntary "shakes" at the mere thought of standing in front of a roomful of people, make sure you can use a lectern, desk, or something to cling to.

○ Take a deep breath before you go to the front of the class. And don't worry about pausing, even taking another deep breath or two, if you lose your place or find your confidence slipping away.

○ If every trick in the world still doesn't calm you down, consider taking a public speaking course (Dale Carnegie, *et al*), joining the Toastmasters Club, or seeking out similar extracurricular help.

COMMON INSTRUCTIONAL VERBS ON ESSAY TESTS

Compare   Examine two or more objects, ideas, people, etc., and note similarities and differences.

Contrast   Compare to highlight differences. Similar to differentiate, distinguish.

Criticize   Judge and discuss merits and faults. Similar to critique.

Define   Explain the nature or essential qualities.

Describe   Convey appearance, nature, attributes, etc.

Discuss   Consider or examine by argument, comment, etc.; debate; explore solutions.

Enumerate   List various events, things, descriptions, ideas, etc.

Evaluate   Appraise the worth of an idea, comment, etc., and justify your conclusion.

Explain   Make the meaning of something clear, plain, intelligible, and/or understandable.

Illustrate   Use specific examples or analogies to explain.

Interpret   Give the meaning of something by paraphrase, by translation, or by an explanation based on personal opinion.

Justify   Defend a statement or conclusion. Similar to support.

Narrate   Recount the occurrence of something, usually by giving details of events in the order in which they occurred. Similar to describe, but only applicable to some thing that happens in time.

Outline   Do a general sketch, account, or report, indicating only the main features of a book, subject, or project.

Prove   Establish the truth or genuineness by evidence or argument. Similar to show, explain why, demonstrate. (In math, verify validity by mathematical demonstration.)

Relate   Give an account of events and/or circumstances, usually to establish association, connections, or relationships.

Review   Survey a topic, occurrence, or idea, generally but critically. Similar to describe, discuss, illustrate, outline, summarize, trace. Some test makers may use these words virtually interchangeably, although one can find subtle differences in each.

State   Present the facts concisely and clearly. May be used interchangeably with name, list, indicate, identify, enumerate, cite.

Summarize   State in concise form, omitting examples and details.

Trace   Follow the course or history of an occurrence, idea, etc.

Writing
with ADD

J ust what is ADD? It's probably easiest to describe as a person's difficulty with focusing on a simple thing for any significant amount of time. People with ADD are described as easily distracted, impatient, impulsive, and often seeking immediate gratification. They have poor listening skills and have trouble doing "boring" jobs (like sitting quietly in class or, as adults, balancing a checkbook). "Disorganized" and "messy" are words that also come up often.

Hyperactivity, on the other hand, is more clearly defined as restlessness, resulting in excessive activity. Hyperactives are usually described as having "ants in their pants." ADHD is a combination of hyperactivity and ADD. According to the American Psychiatric Association, a person has ADHD if he or she meets eight or more of the following paraphrased criteria:

1. Can't remain seated if required to do so.
2. Easily distracted by extraneous stimuli.
3. Focusing on a single task or play activity is difficult.
4. Frequently begins another activity without completing the first.
5. Fidgets or squirms (or feels restless mentally).
6. Can't (or doesn't want to) wait for his turn during group activities.
7. Will often interrupt with an answer before a question is completed.
8. Has problems with chore or job follow-through.
9. Can't play quietly easily.
10. Impulsively jumps into physically dangerous activities without weighing the consequences.
11. Easily loses things (pencils, tools, papers) necessary to complete school or work projects.
12. Interrupts others inappropriately.
13. Talks impulsively or excessively.
14. Doesn't seem to listen when spoken to.

Three caveats to keep in mind: The behaviors must have started before age 7, not represent some other form of classifiable mental illness, and occur more frequently than in the average person of the same age.

CHARACTERISTICS OF PEOPLE WITH ADD

Let's look at the characteristics generally ascribed to people with ADD in more detail:

○ **Easily distracted.** Since ADD people are constantly "scoping out" everything around them, focusing on a single item is difficult. Just try having a conversation with an ADD person while a television is on.

○ **Short, but very intense, attention span**. Though it can't be defined in terms of minutes or hours, anything ADD people find boring immediately loses their attention. Other projects may hold their rapt and extraordinarily intense attention for hours or days.

○ **Disorganization**. ADD children are often chronically disorganized—their rooms are messy, their desks are a shambles, their files are incoherent. While people without ADD can be equally messy and disorganized, they can usually find what they are looking for; ADDers *can't.*

○ **Distortions of time sense**. ADDers have an exaggerated sense of urgency when they're working on something and an exaggerated sense of boredom when they have nothing interesting to do.

○ **Difficulty following directions**. A new theory on this aspect holds that ADDers have difficulty processing auditory or verbal information. A major aspect of this difficulty involves the very common reports of parents of ADD kids who say their kids love to watch TV and hate to read.

○ **Daydreaming**, falling into depressions, or having mood swings.

○ **Taking risks**. ADDers seem to make faster decisions than non-ADDers.

○ **Easily frustrated and impatient**. ADDers do not suffer fools gladly. They are direct and to the point. When things aren't working, "Do something!" is the ADD rallying cry, even if that something is a bad idea.

WHAT PARENTS CAN DO AND SCHOOLS SHOULD DO

What should you look for in a school setting to make it more palatable to a son or daughter with ADD? What can you do at home to help your child (or yourself)? Thom Hartmann offers some solid answers in *Attention Deficit Disorder: A Different Perception*.

○ Learning needs to be project- and experience-based, providing more opportunities for creativity and shorter and smaller "bites" of information. Many "gifted" programs offer exactly such opportunities. The problem for many kids with ADD is that they may be labeled underachieving behavior problems and be effectively shut out of the programs virtually designed for them! Many parents report that children diagnosed as ADD, who failed miserably in public school, thrived in private school, most likely attributable to smaller classrooms, more individual attention with specific goal setting, project-based learning, and similar methods common in such schools. These factors are just what make ADD kids thrive!

○ Create a weekly performance template on which both teacher and parent chart the child's performance, positive and negative.

○ Encourage special projects for extra credit. Projects give ADDers the chance to learn in the mode that's most appropriate to them. They will also give such kids the chance to make up for "boring" homework they sometimes simply can't make themselves do.

○ Stop labeling them "disordered." Kids react to labels, especially negative ones, even more than adults. Saying "you have a deficit and a disorder" may be more destructive than useful.

○ Think twice about medication, but don't discard it as an option. On the other hand, if an ADD child cannot have his or her special needs met in a classroom, not medicating him or her may be a disaster.

SPECIFIC SUGGESTIONS ABOUT WRITING PAPERS

○ Organize your time around tasks. ADDers do well with short bursts of high-quality effort and attention. So, the already-recommended notion of taking a paper and breaking it into a series of far more manageable steps—choose a topic, initiate library research, write first draft—is absolutely essential for ADDers. Such students might find it helpful to break even these steps into a great number of smaller, easily accomplished tasks—breaking "initial library research" into steps like: (1) find pertinent books in card file; (2) find pertinent newspaper articles; (3) read and take notes on first book.

○ Break everything into specific goal units. ADDers are very goal-oriented; as soon as they reach one, it's on to the next. So re-establishing very short-term, "bite-size" goals is essential. Make goals specific, definable, and measurable. Stick to only one priority at a time.

○ Create distraction-free zones. Have them organize their time and workspace to create their own quiet space, especially when they have to write. Have them clean their work area thoroughly at the end of each day. This will minimize distractions as they try to write.

○ Train their attention span. ADDers will probably never be able to train themselves to ignore distractions totally, but a variety of meditation techniques might help them stay focused longer.

INDEX

Notes

Notes

Notes

Notes

Notes

Notes

Notes

Notes

Notes

Notes

Notes

Notes

Notes

Best Selling Series
Over 2 Million
Copies Sold

Ron Fry's
HOW TO STUDY PROGRAM

Ron Fry's best-selling How to Study series is now completely updated and revised to help students meet the increasing demands of the school environment.

What makes the How to Study books so successful?
According to Ron Fry, it's the concepts of time management and organization around which all six books in the series are built. "The keys," says Fry, "are to make the most of the time you have and enjoy what you're doing. It's easier than you think."

About the Author

Ron Fry is a nationally known spokesperson for the improvement of public education and an advocate for parents and students playing an active role in strengthening personal education programs. Aside from being the author of the vastly popular How to Study Series, Fry has edited or written more than 30 different titles — resources for optimum student success.

"Helpful for students of all ages from high school and up."
– Small Press Book Review
"These are must-read guides every family should have in its library."
– Library Journal

How to Study Series

• HOW TO STUDY, SIXTH EDITION
1-4018-8911-5, 2005
264 pp., 5 1/4" x 8 1/4", softcover,

• "ACE" ANY TEST, FIFTH EDITION
1-4018-8912-3, 2005
144 pp., 5 1/4" x 8 1/4", softcover

• GET ORGANIZED, THIRD EDITION
1-4018-8913-1, 2005
144 pp., 5 1/4" x 8 1/4", softcover

• IMPROVE YOUR MEMORY, FIFTH EDITION
1-4018-8914-X, 2005
144 pp., 5 1/4" x 8 1/4", softcover

• IMPROVE YOUR WRITING, FIFTH EDITION
1-4018-8916-6, 2005
168 pp., 5 1/4" x 8 1/4", softcover

• IMPROVE YOUR READING, FIFTH EDITION
1-4018-8915-8, 2005
144 pp., 5 1/4" x 8 1/4", softcover

Ordering Information

To Place an Order please call: (800) 842-3636 *or fax:* (859) 647-5963
Mailing address: Thomson Distribution Center
Attn: Order Fulfillment
10650 Toebben Drive
Independence, KY 41051

SOURCE CODE: CCCSNAH064